Yesterday in the Hills

Yesterday in the Hills

Floyd C. Watkins
and
Charles Hubert Watkins

Foreword by Calvin S. Brown

Brown Thrasher Books
THE UNIVERSITY OF GEORGIA PRESS
Athens

Copyright © 1963 by Floyd C. Watkins and Charles Hubert Watkins
Foreword by Calvin S. Brown copyright © 1973
by the University of Georgia Press
Published as a Brown Thrasher Book, 1982
All rights reserved
Printed in the United States of America
Library of Congress Cataloging in Publication Data
Watkins, Floyd C.
Yesterday in the hills.
"Brown thrasher books."
Reprint. Originally published: Chicago, Quadrangle Books, 1963.
1. Mountain whites (Southern States)—Georgia—Cherokee County. 2. Cherokee
County (Ga.)—Social life and customs. 3. Cherokee County (Ga.)—Biography.
I. Watkins, Charles Hubert. II. Title.
F292.C47W3   306'.09758253   82-2642
ISBN 0-8203-0622-3
ISBN 0-8203-0623-1 (pbk.)

Fourth printing, 2000   ISBN 0-8203-2193-1 (pbk.)

Yesterday in the Hills was first published in 1963 by Quadrangle Books, Inc.,
Chicago. The University of Georgia Press published a new edition in 1973 and
reissued the book in the Brown Thrasher Books series in 1982.

Photograph reproduced from the Collections of the Library of Congress.

Foreword

The past is not an entity, but a trinity. The top layer is the immediate past, which stretches from the evanescent present back to the vague border between childhood and adolescence. This is the period of immediate memories of a time when a man was already essentially himself rather than merely an alien child who would later become himself, for the man of sixty and the boy of twelve are the same in a way that the boy of twelve and the child of six are not. Below the level of this immediate past lies the stratum which is best described as the real past. It embraces the whole period of childhood recollections, and many of these are recollections of things told by parents and grandparents. My father's dog Fido, in 1875, is only a shade less real to me than my own dog Jack, in 1920.

My own real past stretches back to the Civil War because both my grandfathers fought in it and lived to tell the tale. So did the aging veterans, locally known as "the Sons of Rest," who throughout my childhood sat under the trees around the courthouse and embroidered fascinating and incredible tales about it. Thus the Civil War became a part of my real past. But everything before it, from the Carolina parakeet to the brontosaurus, from the New Madrid earthquake to the formation of our galaxy, is lumped together in my historical past. This is the past that is learned from books rather than personal experience or contacts. It can never be quite as real as my real past, and its relative reality depends on the impact of the books rather than the relative closeness of the events described in them. The Trojan

War is more real to me than the American Revolution because it attracted more convincing writers.

Yesterday in the Hills is a venture in the restoration and preservation of the authors' real past. For many rural Southerners on the downhill side of middle age it will function primarily as a stimulus to nostalgic recollection of their own real pasts, and it may well serve its writers' secondary purpose in some such way. This is a legitimate enough function for a book to perform, but it is not the primary purpose of this one, which is basically informative. Those rural Southerners whose own real pasts contain something like what they will find here will enjoy this book, but they will not really need it. Those who need it are the culturally deprived intellectuals who were raised in Fifth Avenue apartments, and urban populations in general, and especially the young, whose real past goes no further back than the first world war. Floyd and Hubert Watkins have set out to portray a vanished way of life which such people know only in the form of crude caricature, and thus to make it a viable part of their historical past. That is why it is being published by a university press.

Whether this is what the writers initially set out to do is irrelevant. Perhaps they merely began to talk over the old times and to record their recollections as retrievements out of the night. Nor does it matter whether the collaboration of son and father was a shrewd calculation or a happy accident. In either case, it provided a highly effective fusion of the immediate past of the father with the real past of the son—a combination which, without interfering with the book's authenticity, somehow provides an effect of esthetic distance.

One or two explanations are in order. The hills referred to in the title are just that—hills. Ball Ground, Georgia, forty miles north of the center of Atlanta, lies at an elevation of a thousand feet, among rolling hills that are beginning to think about becoming mountains, but will have to go some fifteen miles further north before they make up their minds to it. The people are the hill folk of the Piedmont, a different group from the crackers in the pine flats of the coastal plain, south of the fall line. More important, because of the danger of confusion, is the fact that they are also a different breed from the Appalachian mountaineers only a few miles to the north, and that they recognize this difference. There is no hostility between the two groups, but the hill people always refer to "the mountaineers" as outsiders passing through their community. These hill people of North Georgia have more in common with Faulkner's hill people four hundred miles west of them than with the mountaineers thirty miles to the north.

They also lead much the same hard kind of life—but there is no reason for sentimentality about the fact. "Folks that look back at the old times now think it was a hard life," Jess Hudgins tells us, "but then it was just the way of living. . . . But the pore farmer stuck it out, and he didn't know his life was as hard as it was." Subsistence farming, the main occupation, is mixed with day labor and some hunting and fishing and gathering of "wild-food": nuts, berries, etc. Since there is very little actual money, everything that can be is homemade. There are economic differences, but no classes except white and black. Individuality is not only permitted, but esteemed, and the eccentricities of various characters are relished as things that make a rather uneventful life more interesting. The background, education, and values of everyone are so similar that no one sees a difference as a threat.

These common values are important. Most of the hill people are in agreement about the necessity of work, self-reliance, honesty, and charity. The emphasis on the last two of these virtues is well illustrated in the actions of Jess Hudgins's father, who set a bear-trap for a thieving neighbor, caught him, left him in the trap for a while, and then released him, and, realizing that the man was actually hungry, invited him in for breakfast. "The Hopkinses stole corn a lot of times, but they was so needy that nobody wanted to catch them. When they stole something from Pa, he said he guessed it was his turn to make a donation to charity." Religion is generally taken for granted, though it is hard to separate the religious from the social aspects of the activities that center in the church. But there is no spirit of inquisition, and unbelievers are tolerated.

The religious code is, in general, a puritanical one, and its influence is nowhere clearer than in the attitude toward offcolor humor. It is seldom pornographic, but constantly scatological. Many readers will be astonished (though not shocked, in this day and age) by the plainness of speech and the casual occurrence of words usually considered indecent in the speech of these generally puritanical rural people. The explanation is simple: the words are not indecent to them because they know no others. Having neither literary euphemisms nor clinically aseptic terms at their disposal, they use the ancient, basic words for the ancient, basic functions without self-consciousness or too much embarrassment.

There is nothing new, of course, in the description of this sort of simple life, but the approach here is unusual and interesting. Most works which superficially resemble this book are written by local colorists on the one hand or by "social scientists" on the other. The local colorists are almost always sentimentalists on an intellectual slumming tour. They are interested in quaint speech and customs and clothing, often to such an extent that their characters are mere puppets being put through antics that will illustrate the regional idiosyncrasies. The local colorist looks down on his characters by assuming that they exist primarily for the entertainment of his own more sophisticated set. In effect, he winks at his reader and says, "You and I, being far more complicated and sophisticated than these rustics, do not need to take them seriously as persons, but we can be amused and sentimentally moved by their strange carryings-on." For this reason his work is always condescendingly genteel, and usually smugly and offensively so. He is a social snob.

The sociologist and anthropologist, on the other hand, are not sentimentalists, but analysts. But they are also, in their own way, consciously slumming. The local colorists' subjects are simply the raw material for contrived laughter and tears; the social scientists' subjects are the raw material for contrived theories and statistics. These scholars wink at their readers and say, "You and I, being far more intelligent and analytical than these rustics, do not need to take them seriously as persons, but we can take them seriously as classes and explain their strange goings-on—in our own terms, of course, not in theirs." The social scientist is an intellectual snob.

Most accounts of the sort of life here described by the Watkinses and their neighbors have been written by either local colorists or social scientists. In other words, they have been written from the outside. This account shows us the life of the hill people of Georgia from the inside. Hubert Watkins has always lived this life, and Floyd Watkins lived it in his youth. They are not regaling us with the strange goings-on of an alien group, but reliving the life of their own community and people from forty to eighty years ago, reexperiencing it and letting their readers experience it with them. The occasional touches of nostalgia and the necessary explanations here and there are used to make the modern reader at home in their world, not to invite him to look down on it.

It is basically a good world, and we seem gradually and reluctantly to be recognizing this fact. There are far more people now than there were when this book was first published, ten years ago, who realize that the good life cannot be manufactured by technology or created by publicity or legislated by organizations. Such readers will want to think about what they read here, and to think more honestly than the local colorists and more philosophically than the social scientists. They will find entertainment and amusement in the life of a bygone era, and that is as it should be. But some of them, as they read about the way of life of these obsolete hill people—and especially as they meditate on it—may be moved not only to smile at its superficial crudities, but to emulate its fundamental virtues.

April 1973   *Calvin S. Brown*

ix

Acknowledgments

In many ways the hill people themselves have written this book, and we merely held the pen.

Most resemblances to persons, places, and events are entirely intentional. We have changed names and combined and altered persons and events. Those who recognize themselves, we believe, will be pleased with what they are.

We are much obliged to those who helped us remember, especially Frank Watkins, Jim Watkins, Hubert Holbert, Charley Wilkie, Homer Cochran, Clyde Ridings, Calvin Farmer, and Carl Roberts.

We are indebted to Edwin T. Martin and Thomas H. English, who listened and advised; to William B. Dillingham, who read the manuscript; and to the Emory University Research Committee, which provided financial assistance.

Preface

This book began in vague ways and over a period of years, but mainly it started as the attempt of father and son to re-create the past. We wished to describe the day-to-day life and culture of the unlettered Southern hill farmer. The people of the hills (or at least those we knew in the northern half of Cherokee County, Georgia) did not radically change from Reconstruction until World War II. Then most of the older ways disappeared in less than a decade.

But we learned that we could not re-create the old days in all their fullness, because neither writer nor reader can lose his modern perspective. The one-horse farmer of the past cannot be himself as we see him with modern eyes. We can no more go back to his culture than we can become a medieval peasant. A brick house with a bath and a half is also a state of mind. And grandsons cannot think like a grandfather who had never heard of an indoor toilet.

In his own eyes, the hillman was not quaint nor poor nor ignorant nor backward nor even unusual. He was, simply, himself, and he knew what he was in the eyes of himself and his neighbor and his God. He was a student of legend and folklore, but oblivious to history; he lived almost comfortably off the land, but he had no concept of progress; he knew that some families had good blood and rich land and that some families were "trash," but he had no concept of class; he knew that some people lived in cities, but his imagination, which was fertile in comprehending the natural and supernatural worlds, could not conceive of an urban life.

Making a living with the bare hands and a few tools was identity enough. But the next pinnacle beyond survival was personality—the greatest pleasure, the highest aim, and the most significant accomplishment. Individuality was his achievement and his recreation. In the way he planted his crops, voted in an election, told a story, and raised his sons, he set his own standards and spurned all others. Casual in manner but with deliberateness beneath the appearance of ease, he coined his own figures of speech, made up his own jokes, established a reputation as a man of his word, made up his own mind about the character of his neighbors, cultivated his own humor and wit and eccentricity. What the outsider interpreted as backwardness and absurdity, the knowing neighbor viewed as individuality, humor, and companionship.

Contents

THE HOPKINSES

Sam, Donie, Mattie, and Jim Hopkins lived with their folks on the ridge road a mile from the main highway and uphill nearly all the way. Their home, a two-room dilapidated hut, had a moss-covered roof. Mattie was deformed. She had tiny hands and arms and was unable to work.

The Hopkinses had almost nothing to eat. They lived off a little peach orchard and a few crops on a little new ground. In the winter, Ma Hopkins and the girls visited their neighbors a mile away, carried two tow sacks, and filled them with corncobs for their brindle cow. Mattie could not tote cobs, but Donie and her ma carried two partly filled sacks back up the steep road. They boiled the cobs in salty water and fed them to the cow.

The census taker once asked old man Hopkins if there were any idiots in the family. "No, no idiots, I don't reckin," he said; "but there's Jim. When he was a little tad a plowstock fell on his head, and he never has had good sense."

"Well," Jim commented, "plowstock must a fell on the whole damn family."

Once when Hu Watkins went by the Hopkins home before a possum hunt, Donie was churning. Flies covered the sides of the churn, and she caught a handful, "squshed" them to death in her hand, and kept on churning.

Sam was little, and all of his teeth were gone except one large fang, which showed when he laughed. He said he could see better in the dark than the daytime because he was squint-eyed. Sam and his old yellow steer, Buck, tried to farm the hilltops. One year Sam cleared a new ground. When Buck plowed a furrow in the direction away from home, he moved so slow that Sam did not believe they would ever reach the edge of the field. Plowing toward home, old Buck curled his tail and tried to run. When the plow hung under a root in the rough new ground, Sam almost fell over the plowstock. One day Sam unhitched old Buck from the plow and tied him to a sapling to whip him. After three licks, Buck broke loose, hoisted his crooked tail in the air, and rushed over the hill toward home.

Late in the summer Sam pulled fodder with the Watkins boys. They worked until sundown, reached home at eight o'clock, went possum hunting until one or two, rose the next morning before sunup, unloaded the fodder, and went back to the fodder field. Sam's blue-speckled possum dog, Drive, was old and slow on the trail. Sam and his ma and the girls needed the food, and the boys who hunted with him always insisted that he keep the possums. He killed them by pressing a pole across their necks and pulling the possums by their tails until he heard their necks crack. Then he rolled them in steaming wet ashes until the hair slipped off. The women folks baked them in an oven in the open fireplace.

At the neighborhood corn shuckings in the fall, Sam enjoyed the chicken cobbler pie and the other victuals that he could gum and chew with his one big tooth. Most of his days Sam chased after lewd women, but when he was old he finally married. He borrowed $1.50 from Joe Watkins to buy his marriage license. Sam lived with his wife just a few weeks before they separated. Later he cut cordwood to repay the $1.50 he had borrowed to buy the license and joked about the misspent and wasted labor.

When Ma Hopkins died, Sam and the girls went away to the county pauper's home. Over the years they were brought back to the settlement one by one and buried in the Sharp Mountain Church Cemetery.

1

The One-Room School

On the first day of school the Watkins children rose at four-thirty, ate salt mackerel and biscuits and "thickning" gravy for breakfast, fed the mules and hogs and chickens, milked the cows, and dressed in their new clothes. At six o'clock they set out for the school two miles away, crossed the railroad through the stock gates (a fence kept stock off the tracks), and straggled and played up the red clay road over the hills to school. At the bottom of one of the hills was a branch, which was always yellow from the clay and soil washed from the plowed fields. Puzzled by the yellow color, little Hu Watkins dreamed of vast deposits of gold under the earth. He smelled the foul, soured water which ran under a dense growth of cane and brush and wondered why gold caused such an odor.

For half a mile the children walked on a narrow trail through weeds and a field of corn. They smelled the moist earth, the broad rough blades of the corn that overlapped the trail, and the dewy silks on the young "roasenears." Back on the dirt road again, they passed under the sweet-apple tree. Then they walked a quarter of a mile on a trail through the woods. Frank took off his shoes. He had half-soled them himself and driven tacks through the soles without bradding them. The calloused skin on the bottom of his feet looked like the bark of a sweet-apple tree pecked by sapsuckers and peckerwoods.

Flat Bottom School was a wooden box beside a winding dirt road in the north Georgia hills. The summer term began about the second week in July, just after the corn and cotton crops were laid by, hoed and plowed for the last time. Children would not have to work in the fields until fodder-pulling time early in September. For six weeks or two months they were free for education.

A week or two before school began, mothers bought calico cloth to make new dresses for the girls and "check cloth" to make a blue-and-white striped shirt for the boys. "Checks" sold for eight cents a yard at Roberts Store. During the first week of school mothers sewed a second shirt for each boy. These and two pairs of breeches or "overhalls" made up a complete wardrobe for the summer.

The new teacher, Miss Vashti Wilkie, stood on the brush-covered porch of the small schoolhouse, and the children timidly greeted her as they marched into the room and stored their lunches in a safe place. Boys sat on the south side, and the bigger boys made a dash for the back of the room. The seats were long benches made of flat boards. Three pupils sat on the same home-made bench.

Miss Vashti made a short speech. "Good morning, boys and girls," she said. "This makes twenty-two years for me as a teacher in Cherokee County Schools. In all those years I have never seen a group of boys and girls who looked more pleasant than you look this morning.

"Most of you children have finished your work on the crops for the summer, and your folks have made it possible for you to come to school to get an education to help you get along in life when you are men and women. The boll weevil destroys our cotton, and a dry summer makes the crops short, but nothing can take an education away from you.

5

"When you grow up you will be farmers, carpenters, storekeepers, blacksmiths, and teachers, and preachers. Some of you will go on from Flat Bottom School to get higher learning in Ball Ground and Canton, and maybe some of you will go on to college. In school here you ought to try to do something that you will always be proud of and nothing that will make you ashamed."

While she spoke, Barzilla Mulkey looked at Josh Covington and sniggered. Miss Vashti entered all the names in a little book. There were no grades. Every child was classified according to the level of his reader—first-reader, second-reader, and so on. On the first day Miss Vashti spent so much time making assignments that the students did not have to recite. When she called out, "Second class come to the front," they moved to the long benches at the front, watching the new teacher, sizing her up. They marked *begin* and *end* in their books, returned to their seats, and looked at the pictures or forgot the books until she called them for their next class.

Fortunate pupils had five-cent, inch-thick tablets made of paper so rough that it was nearly fuzzy. Pencils were six for a nickel. The rubber on the eraser end was embedded in unpainted cedar wood. Three strokes of erasing and it usually broke. The father often cut each pencil in two with a sharp knife and gave half a pencil to each child. But ten-cent slates in the long run were cheaper; each was about six by eight inches in a wooden frame carved with the owner's initials and made grimy by dirty hands. A slate was a prized possession. When a big boy sat on little Clyde Ridings's slate and broke it, the loss was so great that Clyde remembered his sorrow all his life. The little slate pencils were half as thick as a pencil. They screaked on the slate board and made the students' flesh crawl. Barzilla Mulkey tried to make long and loud noises with his slate pencil and vex the teacher. Students erased by spitting on the slate and rubbing with their fingers or the palms of their hands. On hot days the erasures caused a foul smell in the classroom. But some of the children could not afford to buy even a slate; so they wrote on a small blackboard nailed to the wall.

The major subjects studied in Flat Bottom were arithmetic, reading, writing, spelling, geography, history, and grammar. There were no standard textbooks, and children brought books that had been discarded by an older brother or sister. Students who had no books at all read in their deskmates' books. There were no grades, no report cards, no promotions, no failures; and students were not aware of being slow or fast in their progress from one reader to another. Parents knew nothing about a child's progress except what he told them or what they learned from brothers and sisters. Some teachers lived with the children's parents, moving daily from home to home. Usually the teacher reported that the children were obedient, studious, and loving.

Two or three ages and readers were grouped together when they studied a subject, and the teacher could give only a few minutes to each recitation. Many waited while a few went to the front of the room to recite. Boys and girls twelve to sixteen sat in the same arithmetic class. "Fourth arithmetic class, come to the front," Miss Vashti would say. "Today you were to know the fourth multiplication table." The class spent three or four days in learning one table, and they covered about six lines of the tables during a summer term. While one group recited, other students were supposed to study. But all seventy students, ages five to twenty, could not stay in the small room at the same time, and those above the fourth reader left their books in their desks and played outside when they were not reciting. The teacher called students into the schoolhouse by ringing a bell on the porch or through a window, and a system of signals indicated what group was to come in. Students straggled in from play, stood around the room, and scrooched up several to each desk.

7

At the first of a typical school day, beginners, members of the A-B-C class, were called to the teacher's knee one at a time. Amos Murphy opened his book, and the teacher pointed with her pencil and said, "Now, Amos, what is that letter?"

"That's an A."

"Fine," Miss Vashti said; "you're doing well."

A student in the A-B-C class tried to hold the sound of a letter almost as long as he had breath. "AAAaaaaa," he would say; "BBBBbbbbeeeee, CCCCccccceee," and so on slowly through the alphabet. Some students spent two years in the beginners' group learning their A-B-C's.

In reading classes the students took turns reading aloud. Most of them owned copies of the same book. When a child could not buy a book, the teacher allowed him to use whatever book he had been able to find at home. When a student's turn came, he stood and read a few words, guiding himself by sliding his finger along under each word. When he could not read a word, he stopped and waited for the teacher to prompt him, and then read on until he had to stop again. Brutus Cochran had a complexion like weeds trying to grow under a rotten plank. For his stomach trouble, the doctor had prescribed chewing tobacco. When Brutus read, he chewed vigorously and tobacco juice trickled out of his mouth. But the chewing subsided into misery when he read a poem about a robin and a pussycat.

> Robin Redbreast, sitting in the cherry tree;
> Up went Pussycat; down went he.

When Brutus's moving finger neared the pussycat, he held his finger on the word and looked up to the teacher with wide frightened eyes. The class waited gleefully for the teacher to pronounce the word. She did. But Brutus had to read on:

Up went Pussycat; down went he;
Down went he; up went Pussycat.

Every time Brutus reached the word, he hesitated. Finally the teacher said, "Go on! That word won't bite you." The entire school burst out laughing.

The older students who played outside avoided making enough noise to force the teacher to call them inside. A boundary line divided the playground of the boys from that of the girls. The boys played rough games. Fox and dog races were the favorite sport. A good runner was picked as the fox, and all the others chased him. The fastest hound always threatened to catch the fox in a short race. Toughened by plowing and hoeing from sun-up until sundown, the boys were good runners, and many a chase lasted several miles. The fox who was not caught was a hero.

Girls plaited blades of grass and played house. Boys swung from tree to tree to see how far they could travel without touching the ground. They played nine-men marbles in a square with big earthenware marbles and a center man two inches in diameter. They wrestled, toted over the mark, and fought. The fights were fair, no sticks and rocks, but plenty of fists and skulls. In knuckle kneelings, two boys faced each other and locked their fingers with their arms extended high over their heads, and each tried to force the other to kneel.

Boys and girls played town ball, the country version of baseball. The batter could strike at the ball until he hit it or until he missed and the catcher caught it. A base runner was out if a fielder threw the ball at him and hit him while he was running the bases. Boys tried to throw the ball and hit the bottom of the girls' dresses in a way that would reveal petticoats or an ankle. Odessa Boling had a hard time striking at the ball. She held the bat almost directly in front of her and struck with a downward blow. Ras (Erastus) Bobo would not throw the ball high enough for "Desser" to strike at it over her head. She waited a long time for a ball she could hit, and finally, disgusted, she said, "Throw that-air ball up a little fudder, and I'll hit at hit."

Every boy wished to be some kind of champion. Ras Green was the best knuckle knocker in school; he could hit the side of the schoolhouse with his fist and leave a clear print of four knuckles in the soft old wood. Big-footed Ros (Roscoe) Murphy never wore shoes in the summer. Although one of his toes had been shot off in a hunting accident, he was the fastest runner. Earl Ray could throw a ball harder than any other student. Horace Covington was the champion fighter. Garn (Garnet) Evans was the best cusser. "Ay God," he said, "I've used up all the damned old cuss words and started making me up some new ones. What I'd like to have is a few cuss words so mean the old devil in hell hisself wouldn't want to use em." Josh Covington, a yellow-haired boy with a slick, oily face, always proved his championship at the river on Sundays. After swimming a while, he put his hands and feet on a sandbar and arched his back high. He pumped with all his body, and his belly seemed to operate like an old-fashioned blacksmith bellows. Then after a breathless silence, Josh demonstrated his great accomplishment. He was the settlement's champion wind-breaker.

When the children arrived at school early in the morning, they brought big containers of food for dinner. A family of one or two children had a half-gallon lard bucket with nail holes in the lid so that moisture could evaporate and the food would not become soggy. Three children brought a gallon pail, and big families carried their dinner in a basket. Sometimes older boys carried a separate lunch, usually a biscuit and a piece of salt-cured ham. When the dinner bell rang, the children ran for their food and carried it out where they ate in separate family groups under large trees.

Most of the families brought cornbread, biscuits, boiled roasting ears, ham, or chicken. For dessert they ate pies, gingerbread, teacakes, baked or fried sweet potatoes, or red apples. The yellow horseapples tasted better than the red ones, but the children did not like them as well because they did not look pretty. In the summer when the hens were laying well, students ate great biscuits with fried eggs in the middle. The Murphy boys brought what they called pomegranates, which looked like small golden-colored watermelons or cantaloupes with white stripes. They were not edible, but the girls liked them because of their tart-sweet smell.

Salt mackerel and salmon were delicacies. Pickled in brine, the mackerel came from the store in wooden pails. Ten or fifteen pounds cost no more than sixty-five cents. The mackerel were soaked overnight in water so that part of the salt would dissolve out of them. The student who ate them had to make many a trip to the water bucket, but he felt it was worth it. Sometimes a family ate pink Alaska salmon for breakfast, great quantities fried with flour and meal. The left-overs were packed off to school in the dinner buckets. Sometimes fried salmon smelled up the schoolroom before noon. Cold fried fish, eels, and turtle legs were carried to school more frequently than salmon and mackerel. Cold eel smelled like a stale duck egg. After it was cooked, it swelled bigger and bigger and smelled stronger and stronger. Garn Evans swore that it swelled up one time and blew the top off his lard bucket. Garn did not like salt mackerel because they made him thirsty. One day he held up a little mackerel by its tail and said, "You are a scaly-bellied son of a bitch. You lived in salt water all your sore-headed life, and you'll make me so thirsty I could drink piss-colored muddy creek water."

Josh Covington always had trouble eating fried sweet potatoes. The more he chewed and swallowed, the more the potatoes dammed up in his throat. Then he ate some more, hoping he could push all the potatoes down at once. His eyes bulged out, and his face turned red. Josh said he would get afraid he would burst or die before he could reach the water bucket and the dipper. A big drink of water dislodged the packed potatoes. Josh said, "When them clogged up taters turned loose it felt like Quarleses' Mill Dam had busted loose inside of me."

The food some of the children brought in their buckets was hard on the appetite. Some mothers sent a piece of flabby white sidemeat and bread, or they smeared a little brown sugar on a white gooey biscuit. The Purks family devoured all the lean meat of the hog early in the winter; they had no chickens to fry, no sugar to make pies, no sugar and eggs for cakes, no money to buy salmon and salt mackerel. They had to make out with what they had.

Before the dinner hour on Fridays the teacher often said, "We won't have any books this evening." She meant that the afternoon would be devoted to speeches and games. These exercises were the social highlight of the week for the students and the unmarried young people in the community. Before the dinner bell rang, students watched the road for visitors. Frank Hendrix, a gay bachelor, always came. On hot sunny days, he carried an umbrella to shade himself from the sun under which he had worked hard all week. When he stepped from the dusty road to the school grounds, he stopped, dusted his shining shoes with a weed, and then rubbed them with his handkerchief. He wore blue serge trousers, a tan belt, and galluses. The pleasure-seekers of the community came—Lula and Lena Green; Lilly Hendrix; Richard and David Darby.

When the entertainment began, a pupil said the ninth line of the multiplication table. Frank Hendrix and the audience clapped enthusiastic approval. Then came a prepared debate on a subject such as "Which is the most useful in the home, the broom or the dishrag?" The older boys and girls debated, and each student supported his team by laughing, applauding, and casting triumphant glances at the opponent when a good strong point was made. The visitors served as judges, and when the decision was announced half the school jumped wildly with joy. Two students chose sides for a spelling bee, and the teacher gave out words from the old *Blueback Speller.* When a student missed a word, he sat down. There was glory for the winning side, and the last pupil standing was the hero of the day.

Speeches and poems were always popular. Big boys slouched to the front of the room and said little poems:

> Here I stand on a punkin.
> Come and kiss me, sugar dumplin.

Or:

> A B C, dominecker dee.
> Cat's in the cupboard and can't see me.

Or:

> Up the hickory
> Down the pine.
> Tore my breeches
> Right behind.

Or:

> Squirrel in the bushes
> Squirrel on the ground.
> Hey, little squirrel,
> Why don't you come down?
> I step back;
> My gun crack;
> Down come little squirrel
> Flat of its back.

Or:

> Possum up a simmon tree,
> Raccoon on the ground.
> Raccoon says to the possum,
> Shake them simmons down.

Or:

> A chicken's feet
> And a chicken's gizzard,
> My sweetheart's
> Slick as a lizard.

Timid little girls blushed when they recited:

> Roses are red;
> Violets are blue.
> Sugar is sweet
> And so are you.

A pupil who wished to annoy his teacher spoke out loud and clear:

> I had a little dog.
> His name was Rover.
> Every time he died,
> He died all over.
> All but the end of his tail,
> And it turned over.

Jim Bice, one of the most reckless of the boys, risked saying this one:

> I had an old mule, and his name was Jack.
> Tied him on the railroad track.
> Along came a train, toot—toot—toot.
> Old Jack, he went poot—poot—poot.

A favorite game was Laugh and Go Foot. The boys formed into a line facing a line of girls. One Friday, Jess Hudgins told each boy what to say to the girl opposite him, and Lucy Bobo planned the remarks of the girls. Any student who laughed at a ridiculous comment had to move to the foot of the line. Sim Walker was at the head of the line, and he was so weak-eyed that matter, or "cracklings," gathered in the corners of his eyes. Frony Hudgins was supposed to say something to Sim, and she was nervous and bashful. Lucy whispered to her, and Frony said, "You're so sweet the sugar is running out of your ass." She meant to say "eyes." The children laughed so much that school had to break up for the day.

Punishment in Flat Bottom School was a hard whipping with a long hickory or withe, but good teachers did not have to punish often. Students watched the whippings and then tried to avoid getting one themselves. Occasionally, some country school succeeded in running a weak teacher out of the settlement, but this never happened at Flat Bottom. Once on the first day of school Jim Bice kicked a big fat new teacher in the belly, but after the whipping Jim never was so brave again. John Drummond, a tall and thin man with enormous gold teeth, decided that he needed an education when he was forty years old. He enrolled in Flat Bottom and attended the same school with several of his children. He was in a grade lower than one of his boys. John enjoyed his second childhood. When he misbehaved, Miss Vashti made him stand on one foot in the corner of the schoolroom. Sam Worley once slipped up behind some of the girls and scratched their necks with a prickly chestnut bur. They told the teacher, Paul Abbott, a pale, thin, black-haired man. When Mr. Abbott tried to talk to Sam, he fought the teacher; they beat and choked and scratched each other. Sam won the fight, but the students sided with the teacher and Sam quit school.

Mr. Abbott chewed tobacco and kept a can to spit in while he was teaching. Bill Compton, a student in the fourth reader, kept a thirty-eight pistol in his desk several days before it was discovered and reported to the deputy sheriff, Jess Bassett. Jess locked Bill up in the district jail house. When the justice of the peace asked Bill why he had a pistol in his desk, Bill replied, "To make the others study their lessons, and to keep them from throwing spit balls."

Lije (Elijah) Compton threatened to give Mr. Wiley a beating. "Now, boys," he would say, "it's going to be rough on the little fessor if he tries to boss me." The crisis came. The small teacher called Lije to the front of the room and began shaking his finger in his face. Lije held a clenched fist behind him for all the students in the room to see. The teacher looked weak and helpless, and the students were scared. Then Mr. Wiley saw the fist. He swung quick and hard and sprawled Lije flat on the floor. He wilted like a green crisp head of lettuce dipped into boiling water.

Generally the teachers ruled benevolently and firmly. But they had to be shrewd to catch some culprits. One winter term red-headed Jim Bice wrapped rifle cartridges in paper and dropped them into the heater. When a cartridge exploded, the students thought the schoolroom had blown up. It was weeks before Miss Vashti Wilkie caught him. She sent for a hickory, and the student returned with a switch as long as the teacher. When Jim came to the front to receive his punishment, he looked like a giant standing beside a threatening midget. Miss Vashti started with blows on his broad back; her face became red and the blows became harder. Just as the hickory landed each time, she rose up on her tiptoes.

Like other parents in the community, Jim's father, old Bill Bice, supported the teacher. When Jim and his brothers and sisters reached home, his least sister, Bessie Mae, said, "Pa, Jim got a whupping today."

"What'd you git the whupping fer, Jim?"

"Aw, Pa, I just drapped a few little old catterges in the heater to hear them pop. That's all."

"You know I've always told you that when you git a whupping at school I'm gonna give you the same number of licks at home. Bessie Mae, you go git me a withe off the peach tree. I hope you didn't fergit to count the licks, Jim."

A few teachers had been to college; some had finished only the seventh or the ninth grade. Anyone who could pass an examination given by the county school superintendent was given a license to teach. The salary was thirty to forty dollars a month for five months a year, a fairly high wage for the time and place. The teacher was highly respected as a man of mind and character in the settlement. Men asked for his opinion about politics and world affairs. He dressed well—a homemade white shirt, no tie, dark blue-serge trousers, suspenders, and polished high-top black shoes.

After the first day of school in the summer boys wore three pieces of clothes: a wide-brimmed straw hat, knee-length breeches or "overhalls," and a checked shirt. In the winter boys and girls wore long union-suit underwear, and the girls tucked the long legs into their stockings all the way down to their high-top shoes. Clothes were cheap, but money was dear. When Tom Spence, the son of the local drunk, was wrestling on a cold winter day, his shirttail came out. The other students shivered with pity when they saw that he wore no underwear. Old grannies told tales of children being sewed up in their underwear from the first frost of the fall until it was cut off them and burned in the spring, but this fashion had vanished before the twentieth century. The girls' hair hung down their backs in plaited pigtails. A boy did not comb his hair until he was old enough to court the girls. When there were epidemics of lice, some mothers washed their children's hair with home-

17

made lye soap. Most boys took a bath occasionally; some, every spring; and some, only when they were born. For some, the smell of soured sweat was a prized symbol of hard work.

On the last day of the term the teacher distributed candy, a red stick at a time to lined-up pupils until the three or four boxes of candy were empty. The Hopkins children were the poorest in the community, and Miss Vashti Wilkie gave them twice as many sticks as she gave the others. Some pupils understood, but a few were resentful.

The summer school term always ended with a grand outdoor entertainment. Students carried benches outdoors, made more seats from sawmill slabs nailed to stumps, and brought chairs from home. Possum hunters' lanterns and kerosene lamps provided light. Miss Vashti pumped the organ with her feet and accompanied the audience as they sang religious songs. John W. Hendrix, a chubby middle-aged man with a short black mustache, recited a long comical speech about "My Gal Sal." For years and years he said the same speech at most social gatherings. Everyone enjoyed it—over and over.

The teacher, Miss Vashti, had taught Hu Watkins a speech. Every day for three weeks she had listened to the students' speeches. "Now," she had told Hu over and over, "be sure and talk loud enough." When the great occasion arrived, he overcame his shyness and hollered as loud as a possum hunter.

> When I'm a man I mean to be
> A boxer bold, as you will see;
> I'll send opponents to the ground
> And beat them in the seventh round.

Hu did not know the meaning of *boxer, bold, seventh round,* and *opponent.* All he understood was "When I'm a man." He never asked the meaning of the words, and no one bothered to tell him. Years later he learned the meaning of what he had said. Forty-seven years later he attended a reunion of Flat Bottom alumni, and Julia Murphy told him that she remembered his speech, and she said it perfectly.

Children who had spent the late spring and early summer working hard in the fields looked forward to school as a time of relaxation and some foolishness and horseplay. Some children went to school only because they hoped to have a good time or because their parents made them go. Some studied hard and struggled for the best education they could get. When the summer term was over, they harvested the crops. After the cotton was picked and the corn was gathered, they walked to school in Ball Ground and entered two months after all the town children had started. They struggled to catch up in their studies, walked miles to school, waded over muddy roads without raincoat or umbrella, and carried lunches in a lard bucket. When spring plowing began, they quit two months before school was out and went back to work in the fields.

JAUNY LOOMIS

When the regular preacher finished his sermon at Locust Grove Church, Jauny Loomis pushed himself into the pulpit. The people had a hard time trying to stop his preaching without causing a fuss, but Jauny finally had to quit after he tried to use too many big words in his sermons. He preached against making and drinking whisky and called over the different names that show how bad it is—booze, killemquick, white-lightning, rotgut, and popskull. Then he yelled, "I've even heared some of the boys say, 'Let's go to Atlanter and git us some poontang.'" When Jauny finished his sermon, he asked a young lady, Precious Hester, to come up and urinate on the organ as the congregation sang.

One fall Jauny collected wasp nests, covered them with a little honey, and tried to sell them as honey. The merchant Webb Roberts sold sorghum from a barrel. One of his sons failed to put the bung in the bunghole after he sold a gallon of syrup one day, and several rats scrambled into the sorghum barrel and drowned. Webb gave old Jauny the syrup to feed his hogs. He hauled it home, strained the rats out, and carried it back to town and sold it to Webb as fresh syrup. When Webb learned what Jauny had done, he cussed him so thoroughly that Jauny was afraid to return to town for a month.

Luke Gibbs once took up a collection for Jauny in the marble mill. He asked for a quarter from every man. Jauny had been gassed while he was digging a well, Luke said, and he could not sit down. All he could do was "hunker around a chair." The marble workers gave a quarter apiece, and then they learned that Luke had caught Jauny stealing his firewood. He could not sit down because Luke had shot him in the rear while he was stooping over. After that, Luke had a hard time collecting for charity in the mill.

Jauny was the stingiest man in the settlement. He bought a pair of size-twelve shoes, although he should have worn nines. He said he wanted to get his money's worth of leather when he had his shoes half-soled. Neighbors said that Jauny gave his children a penny to go to bed without supper, stole the penny while they were sleeping, and tried to give it to them again the next night. At night Jauny and his wife turned the kerosene lamp off to save money, and he sat with his breeches off to keep from wearing out the seat of his pants. He caught lightning bugs in the summer and used them for a lamp. Thread at Roberts Store sold for five cents a spool, and Jauny asked old man Webb if he would sell him two spools for nine cents. He carried acorns in his pocket and gave them to tumblebugs when he stole their piles. The neighbors said that Jauny hoped even a tumblebug would not know it when Jauny cheated him.

2

Sharp Mountain Church

Early in the morning of the first Sunday of each month in the Sharp Mountain settlement, Christians and non-Christians began to get ready to go to church. The family ate a special Sunday breakfast, fed the stock, put on their Sunday best, and traveled over dusty or muddy roads on foot, in buggies and wagons to Sharp Mountain Church. Good churchmen had already attended a business meeting of the congregation and heard a long sermon on the Saturday before the Sunday meeting. Frank Hendrix walked to church, holding an umbrella over his head to shade himself from the hot sunshine. He walked in front of his horse and buggy, and his wife and his aged mother rode. When he arrived at the church, he always carefully hitched his horse to the same oak tree.

There was no Sunday school. People gathered on the church grounds, and one neighbor greeted another: "Howdy, Nathan, how are you all?"

"Oh, just tolable, Peter. How're you folks? Is Mandy able to be up and about?"

At 10:30 Brother Frank Hendrix, the song leader, came to the door and announced in a loud voice, "Everybody come in, and we'll sing a few songs."

The old and the faithful and the enthusiastic went

inside, but many boys stayed under the shade of the trees, and boys and girls continued to talk and court in the buggies and wagons.

Sometimes the pastor talked from eleven in the morning until the "evening" train went down at three o'clock. Usually a sermon lasted two hours. Visiting preachers (as many as four) sat behind the pastor on the elevated preacher's stand. After the pastor finished his sermon, each visitor "offered a few words"—enough to last for at least thirty minutes each. They preached in relays— each until he was tired. While the sermons went on and on, some stragglers wandered inside, and the impatient rose and slipped out of the church. But the faithful and the patient held their eyes on the preacher. Babies on their mothers' laps fretted and cried. A water bucket with a gourd dipper sat close to the pulpit. During the services children and adults walked up to the front and took a drink of water. Restless and hungry children hunted for sweetbread in the mothers' satchels. Babies slept on quilts spread out on the floor.

As soon as the congregation was dismissed on foot-washing days, the married folks began to prepare their big Sunday dinner on the grounds. The young men who were sitting and talking outside underneath a tree and the boys and girls who were courting in wagons and buggies began a stroll to the spring about a quarter of a mile from the church. The boys walked ahead on a trail through the woods, and the girls followed. At the spring, the boldest boy of the group filled a gourd with a drink of water and took it to one of the girls. Then others in turn carried water to the girls. As they started back toward the church, a boy walked up to a girl and asked, "Will you accept my company?" Sometimes she said, "Yes, sir." Often she said, "No"; then the boy received what he called a "slighting." Backward and timid George Jordan once summoned all his courage, walked up to Sally Brown, and asked her to walk with him. When she said

"No," his world fell apart. Many boys never dared to ask a girl to walk back from the spring to the church. They were too bashful and scared.

When the young folks returned from the spring, the women had set vast quantities of food on the long plank tables. Palestine (or "Pally") Watkins's family brought an old-fashioned, oval-top trunk full of food for the twelve in the family. They hauled it to church with Old Charley, and then one of the children led the gray horse and the buggy back to the barn. When they hitched him at church, he always broke loose and ran away. Every mother brought the best she could afford: fried chicken, salt-cured ham, fish, baked hen, boiled eggs, country-fried steak, cornbread, biscuits, homemade loaf bread, beans, peas, tomatoes, cantaloupe, watermelon, tarts and pies and cakes of every shape and flavor. Moving from table to table, the people ate food from as many different homes as they could. Dinner was late, the people worked hard, and they ate enough to help them to plow for a week. Mothers tested their ability as cooks by the number of visitors to their tables, and they tried to persuade every passer-by to have something to eat. When the men had stuffed as much as they could, they fed corn and bundles of fodder to their horses and mules, and then they moved under the trees to rest. The mothers stacked the plates, and the children played.

A half-hour after dinner Brother Hendrix again came to the door and said, "Come in, and let's sing awhile." Twice a year, in May and September, it was foot-washing day. Communion preceded the washing of feet. A large glass of blackberry wine passed slowly around the congregation, each member taking a sip. After old Herb Prince's wildest boy drained a full glass, Herb took him out to a pine thicket and whipped him. Herb himself took several good drams every day, but he was serious about his religion.

After communion, the deacons began noisily preparing

for the foot-washing, gathering the towels and clinking the shiny tin washpans. The women all sat on the right side of the church, and the men on the left. Brother Jim Holcomb tied a white towel around himself and asked Brother Noble Goss for the opportunity of washing his feet. Brother Goss accepted; he sat down on a bench and put his feet one at a time into the big washpan. Brother Holcomb washed Brother Goss's feet with his hands and dried them carefully with the towel. Then Brother Goss and Brother Holcomb stood up, vigorously shook hands, and exchanged places. After Brother Goss washed Brother Holcomb's feet, they stood up again and enjoyed a more prolonged handshake. Everyone followed the same ritual.

Once General Wheeler (*General* was his first name, not a title) forgot that it was foot-washing day until he was crossing a branch close to Sharp Mountain. Then he remembered. His feet were dirty; on the way to church he had helped a neighbor catch a hog that had been running free in the fields. He told his wife Callie that he believed in washing feet, that he was going to take part in the service, and that he did not wish to let any church brother wash his feet while they were dirty. Callie held General's mule, and he went down among the bushes and briars to the branch and washed his feet.

As the foot-washing progressed, the happy emotions increased. Nearly always at about the second or third round Sister Hudgins started the shouting and Sister Wilkie followed. Preacher Stephens began to sing, "We have fathers over yonder; we have mothers over yonder, and we'll soon go there to see them." Sister Vashti Wilkie moved about over the house, shouting and clapping her hands and chanting, "Yes, we have loved ones over yonder, and we are going there to see them." Many of the women were transported in an emotional ecstasy. After Hu Watkins's mother Palestine died, Sister Vashti always shouted her way to him at the foot-washings. "Now your mother's in that glory land!" she would say. "Aren't we happy!" The preacher continued his solo in a lonely voice: "We have fathers over yonder; we have mothers over yonder." He sang old-fashioned lonesome songs that made children think they were hearing a suffering spirit wailing in sorrow. Aunt Rachel Doss always wore a little black bonnet which hung down over her shoulders and protruded out in front of her face. She shouted quietly and softly, clapped her hands, and jumped up and down. Aunt Emmer Green shouted with a great exuberance. Her shaking made her hairpins fall to the floor, her long hair covered her face, and she had to feel her way about through hair and tears to beat her good fellow Christians on the back.

Men seldom shouted. Aunt Clary Thomas always said that men do not resist temptations very well and that they find it hard to get that shouting feeling. But old Peter Cowart was a great shouter. Once in August when he and his wife were attending church during the summer revival, a summer cloud came up while old Peter was in the middle of his shouting. Their turnip patch at home was ready to sow. When it began to thunder, Peter's wife went to him as he was shouting, took his arm, pulled him down, and whispered in his ear, "Peter, hit's a coming up a cloud. We had better go home and sow our turnips before the rain gits here." He stopped shouting, listened carefully, then raised up and yelled, "Turnips or no turnips, I'm going to serve my Lord."

About the time of the laying by of the crops in July, Sharp Mountain Church began talking about a revival or protracted meeting. Pastor Stephens and the deacons believed in waiting for the Spirit to move them before they set a date. About the first Sunday in July, Preacher Stephens said it was time for a revival and asked the members to be alert to the calling of the Spirit. But the Spirit always seemed to be slow in naming a time.

Usually fodder pulling had started before the revival began.

One service was held at eleven o'clock in the morning, and about sundown families began gathering for the second meeting of the day. In buggies and wagons and afoot they came early to talk with neighbors and kinfolk and to court their sweethearts. Just before dark the preacher came to the door and shouted in a loud bass voice, "It's time to begin." Mothers entered the church toting one baby in their arms and leading another by the hand. One of the larger children carried a satchel of sweetbread to pacify the children when they beċame tired, hungry, and restless. Another child brought a jar of water. Some mothers spread an old quilt on the floor for the smallest children to lie on and sleep. Brother Hendrix began singing "Revive Us Again," and by the time the second verse started the church was full and the congregation was in a singing mood.

After several songs, Preacher Stephens pulled off his coat, drank water from the gourd and bucket in front of the preacher's stand, and began his sermon. He warned sinners to repent of their sins and to come to the Lord. He pled with church members who had strayed to change their way of living. He preached of the great judgment day when saints would go through the pearly gates to the streets of gold and when the sinners would be cast into outer darkness and lakes of fire and brimstone, where there would be weeping and wailing and gnashing of teeth.

Sweat and tears poured down the preacher's face, and his shirt clung to his skin. He preached at the top of his voice, then spoke of the horrors of hell in a terrifying and menacing whisper. After a long sermon by the pastor, a visiting preacher also preached to the sinners.

Preacher Bell was called the cyclone preacher and the rafter rattler. When his turn came, he slowly pushed himself onto the elevated pulpit, took a drink of water, cleared his throat, and looked about over the congregation. He started slow and quiet. After a while he made contact with the Spirit, plopped his hand on the stand and his foot on the floor, and in a loud cry finished the sentence that had begun quietly. The worshipers shifted a little and opened their eyes wide. Preacher Bell became a fury of motion. He slung his long arms, clapped his calloused, bony hands, jumped up and down, leaned forward and then backward, and talked faster and louder. When he reached the highest pitch the windows and doors rattled. Children expected the board shingles to fly off the top of the church.

Finally the time came for the invitation hymn. The congregation sang "Just as I Am Without One Plea," and sinners were invited to come to the mourners' bench. Many came down the aisle, gave the preacher their hand, fell prostrate on the bench, and wept with loud cries of anguish. The singing continued, and Preacher Stephens pled with sinners between stanzas, sang the hymn, and chanted his pleas between phrases of the music. Brothers and Sisters fanned the mourners, patted them on the back, pled with them, and asked them to give up and to accept the Lord's forgiveness of their sins. After a time someone started singing "Lord, I'm Coming Home." A mourner would jump to his feet and grab the Christian nearest to him. Sister Doss, Brother Mulkey, and old Aunt Marthy Scott shouted and praised the Lord; others moved through the congregation, pleading with the unsaved sinners to come to the bench. More sinners rose from the bench with beaming faces and loud praise for the Lord. The cries of the damned mingled with shouts of joy of the recently saved.

One summer a severe dry spell almost burned up the crops of the community. Old Brother Bell always said that in years of disaster folks wake up to their need of the Lord, and that year many sinners came to the mourners' bench. Buck Mullinax came to the mourners' bench every revival for many years. Once he became so interested in the proceedings that he forgot his own sin and his mourning, raised his face from his elbow, and watched the commotion around him. But the next revival Buck was saved. He joined the church and became a good church member. The wife of Preacher Wilkins went to the mourners' bench as a sinner for more than forty years; finally she joined the church and declared in her testimonial that she had been converted when she was a girl.

When Gid Wheeler's mother, Clea, took him to Sharp Mountain Church and he heard the mourners crying and moaning, he asked, "Mama, what's the matter with em?"

"Ah, son," she explained, "they don't want the boogerman to git em."

A few moments later Gid saw Joe Prince with his long black beard and said, "Oh, Mama, looky yonder. He's come to git em."

For many years the widower Joe Mullinax wept on the mourners' bench during revivals and bootlegged mountain moonshine whisky during the rest of the year. Again and again he was caught by revenue officers. Joe was always busy, serving sentences in the jail, crying on the mourners' bench, making and selling whisky, and making trips to the red-light district in Atlanta. Once he became afflicted with a venereal disease. He returned to the whorehouse, found the girl and told her, "Damn you, you give me the clap." She said, "I gave you the clap, hell; you paid me two dollars for it." Later he married a second wife and raised several children; most of them were deaf and dumb. In his late forties Joe became a church member and lived a good life.

Revivals ended on Sunday with a great crowd of people gathering at the Etowah River under the bridge just below the Quarles Mill Dam. The people stood under the shade of sycamore trees between the canebrake and the river bank, and the preacher preached for half an hour. Then he said, "All you candidates for baptism gather here together to go into the water to be baptized." As the congregation sang "On Jordan's Stormy Banks I Stand," the preacher took the hand of one of the converts, and the candidates joined hands and formed a chain. They walked slowly out into the deeper water in the middle of the river. First the women were baptized. The younger girls seemed afraid of the cold water that flowed down from the mountains. The preacher placed his left hand over the chest of the candidate, raised his right hand heavenward, and said, "I baptize you, my sister, in the name of the Father, the Son, and the Holy Ghost." Then he dipped the candidate below the surface of the water. Many came up shouting the praises of the Lord, and those on the banks chanted Amens. Once Mary Keith, a big fat woman, went to a baptizing wearing a brand new Sunday hat with big red roses on top. As each one of the women rose from the watery grave, Mary became happier and happier. Finally she yelled, "I'm gonna shout or bust wide open." Then she tenderly took the hat from her head and handed it to Hanna Gilmer, "Here, Hanna, you hold my hat. I'm a gonna get in that air shouting." At one baptizing in late August the first woman baptized came up out of the water, popped her hands, and happily exclaimed, "I love everbody." The second one hollered, "I feel like I could scale the walls of Jericho." The third yelled, "Christmas gift to everbody."

After the boys and the men were baptized, the new Christians walked slowly out of the water in their dripping clothes, and the people on the bank sang "Shall We Gather at the River?" Then the women went to the old mill house to change their clothes, and the men changed in a nearby thicket of bushes and vines. From the river the congregation went to the church for the rest of the ceremonies. There those who had been baptized lined up in the front of the church to receive the right hand of church fellowship. The members of the church formed a long line to march by and shake the hands of the newly saved. Happy and exuberant shouting at times almost drowned out the sound of joyful hymns.

The pastor of Sharp Mountain Church served without pay. It would have been evil to pay him, the members believed, and sinful on his part to accept any money. For years and years the church had no musical instrument of any kind; musical accompaniment, the congregation believed, was inappropriate to the simple religion of the Bible. When a hymn began, five or six song leaders hummed to set the key, and the congregation began to sing. A child younger than twelve years old never went to the mourners' bench nor joined the church; Jesus Christ, the people said, did not participate in religious activities before He was twelve. The pastor taught that bobbed hair for women was evil, and many feared to disobey the Old Testament admonition against the buying and selling of dogs.

Women were allowed to shout or to make testimonials, but they were not permitted to speak in business sessions. Donie Mulkey had something she wished to say about church affairs almost every meeting. She had to go outside, talk with two deacons, and register her complaint or make her suggestion through them. Women never prayed aloud in the church. Some veiled themselves with black bonnets in public. Pastor Stephens's wife attended church services for decades, but some of her husband's close friends would not have recognized her if they had seen her without her bonnet. She kept her face hidden, and never did she speak a word to one of the men in the church. Occasionally she did whisper softly to a woman neighbor sitting nearby.

The church had two front doors. Men entered through the door on the left and sat on the left side, and women

31

entered and sat on the right. Husbands and wives never sat together. No man ever entered the right door except when he was with his girl. Sometimes a boy and his girl sat together in the middle row of the rough wooden benches. It was scandalous for a young couple to attend a funeral together. The congregation especially objected when a girl and a boy walked together up to the coffin to view the corpse. A funeral was too solemn for anything like courting.

Funerals were almost always held at eleven o'clock. There were no undertakers, no embalming. Friends of the family of the dead laid out the corpse. Gordon Covington was a sort of amateur undertaker. He laid out more male corpses than anyone in the settlement. His wife Alice usually helped with the women. Often in the summer the odor of the decaying body in the hot church was almost unbearable. Funerals seemed to be almost a pleasant recreation to some of the more sentimental women of the neighborhood. The family's love was measured by the noise of the weeping, by the "taking on," as the mourning was called. When a child returned home from a funeral, his brothers and sisters who had not gone asked him, "Did they take on a whole lot?" Then he tried to describe the hollering and fainting.

Wimpy Pearson was a problem to the churches in several settlements. He attended nearly all the revivals in the summer and tried to join the church during every revival. When a deacon asked him why he wanted to join so many churches so often, he said, "When the spirit starts working in the congregation and the singing starts, I just feel so good that I have to do something about it. I remember how I was so happy the last time I jined, and I jist want to jine agin. I shore do enjoy being baptized."

If a member of the church sinned and did not acknowledge his evil ways publicly, a deacon or a member of the congregation brought charges against him, and usually he was turned out of the church. Drunkenness and cursing were the most common causes of expulsion. Young people were turned out of the church for dancing or for playing music for a dance. A girl who had an illegitimate baby was ousted. Cowline (Caroline) Mulkey married, separated, divorced, and then married Sam Reece. The church had a great argument over doctrine as a result of the charges against her. Some members maintained that she was living in adultery with Sam. Preacher John Bell became so angry that he threatened to hit Sam's brother, Tom, with a walking stick. Mrs. Reece was turned out of the church, but she continued to attend, and finally she was quietly accepted again as a member.

Once there was a dispute about the conduct of the Darby girls with young men. The father, old Lum Darby, protested that his girls had not done anything wrong. Deacon Jake Ponder, who made the accusations, became so angry that he wished to fight, and members of the congregation thought that he was as sinful as the girls. Sometimes the church turned people out for taking part in the services of another denomination. Lint Gazaway was turned out after he attended a revival in the Holy Roller Church. Later Lint acknowledged his sin, and they took him back into the church. Even after the church had electric lights, Lint always brought his lantern with him. On the night when he was readmitted, he waved his lantern, clapped his hands, stamped his feet, and shouted that he was a lamb returned to the fold.

Shortly after 1900, the Reverend Josiah Scruggs, a preacher from Alabama, came into the settlement and began a revival. The entire community was shaken by his thunderous preaching about hellfire and damnation. Great numbers of sinners flocked to the mourners' bench, and seventy-seven were converted and baptized. Later the congregation learned that the Reverend Scruggs had been caught fondling a girl on the mourners' bench in a church in Alabama. His church had deprived him of the right to preach. The new members who had been baptized by Scruggs were turned out of Sharp Mountain Church unless they consented to be baptized again by an acceptable preacher. Some were baptized again, but some refused. The association of Baptist churches approved of the Scruggs baptisms, and some of the converts moved to other churches. In a sawmill metaphor the association branded Sharp Mountain the "slab-off outfit." For years thereafter Sharp Mountain was an independent church which belonged to no association of churches.

Old Uncle Joe Starnes, a lay preacher, announced that he would preach a sermon about the dissension. He began at midday and preached about the troubles in the church until sundown. Then the Slab-offs decided to close the church to the other faction. They padlocked the log building and locked a heavy log chain around one of the big fourteen-inch logs and through a large auger hole in the door. Granny Mary Brown Watkins, a sister of Governor Joseph E. Brown, did not believe the Lord's house should be padlocked. She carried her ax to the church and chopped off the chain as she sang "Work for Jesus." But Granny could not stop the trouble; she joined a church in Ball Ground, and the fuss just gradually wore itself out.

The earliest death date on a tombstone in the Sharp Mountain cemetery is 1842, but earlier graves are probably unmarked and lost. Negroes attended Sharp Mountain Church with the whites until 1912; they sat in the extreme back of the church on the right. About 1912 they were run out of the settlement after news that a Negro had raped a white woman in an adjacent county. Even after that, some Negro funerals were held in Sharp Mountain Church. In 1918 white and black attended the funeral of Pete Jordan, a favorite with both races. A Negro preacher preached, and Mrs. Hallie Minch, a white woman, told how Pete had been a great friend to her and her family. Pete was buried with nickels on his eyes to keep them closed. Because of that old custom, a child in the old days would have placed a live coal of fire in his mouth in preference to a nickel.

Time changes the graveyard a little. Foam crosses and red and green plastic flowers decorate the newer graves, but the raw red clay slowly sinks back to the natural level. Weeds and the natural growths of the hills struggle to cover the old graves. A few mounds have disappeared forever.

BEDNEY HOLCOMB

*Abednego Holcomb lived on a farm on the Etowah
River in the Conn's Creek settlement. He and his first
wife raised twelve children. Uncle Bedney sent all his
children to school and took them to church. When his
wife died, his neighbors worried about how he would
take care of his children, and some of the wits wondered
how the settlement would keep the school attendance
up. The population, they feared, would drop off at an
alarming rate because no one could be as good as Uncle
Bedney and his wife in populating the community.*

*All the problems were solved when Uncle Bedney
married a young woman. Over the years they had
eleven children. In all, Uncle Bedney had twenty-three
children. Every one of them married, and when there
was a family reunion Uncle Bedney's grandchildren
did not know many of their forty-four uncles and aunts
and their hundreds of first cousins. Uncle Bedney
taught all his children to work hard, to be honest, and
to do their part in the community. The children scattered from South Carolina to Texas. They became
farmers and merchants, traders and preachers and
teachers, and the neighbors said that not a one of them
did anything that Uncle Bedney should have been
ashamed of. When Uncle Bedney died, they carved
his name and the one word FATHER on his tombstone,
and the neighbors said that he had earned his epitaph.*

3

The Hudgins Family

(As Remembered and Told by Jess Hudgins)

A feller who growed up on a farm in the hills never forgot his raising. Just about everything he had was homemade. It was a homemade life.

Some families had log houses, but ours was weatherboarded. Pa built it the first winter after he married when he didn't have to work in the fields. He cut down enough pine trees for lumber and to pay the sawmill man for sawing the boards. He run the boards straight up and down and overlapped them to keep out the wind and the rain. He hauled rocks and made rock pillars to keep the house off the ground. The house didn't have underpinning, and dogs and hogs crawled under it to be warm in the winter and cool in the summer. Ma's hens made nests back where the sills almost touched the ground, and us children crawled under the house to hunt for eggs and to play. My sister Lucy always run under the house to get away from Ma's switch. One time after she got big and fat she got stuck way back under the house and Rufe had to come in from the field to help her get loose.

When Pa was young, nails cost too much for most folks to buy; a man put his house together with wooden pegs or homemade nails made by the blacksmith. Most of the money spent on a house went for nails and winder

panes. The chimney was made of rocks and red mud. Pa
rived shingles from short lengths of red-oak logs. He built
a front piazzer where he could rest in the summer and
pile his cotton in the early fall and his firewood in the
winter. Ma kept the bare clay yard swept clean with a
brush broom. They was oak and hickory trees in the
yard, but not enough to keep us from seeing the traffic
passing by on the dirt road in front of the house.

The homemade doors had a latch on the inside and a
string run through a hole to the outside. Pa and Ma
always was telling people, "Come to see us. The latch-
string is on the outside." The door had a cathole. Polecats went in and out of the cathole at Sam and George
Freeman's house, and them two old bachelors petted the
polecats just like housecats. Sam said they made the best
rat-catchers they ever was. Our front door opened up to
a hall which run between the bedrooms to the back
porch. Some houses didn't have doors at either end of
the hall. They was just open. The hall was a cool
place to set in the summer, but in winter we nearly froze
as we run from the fire through the open hall to the
sleeping rooms. Sometimes snow blowed into the house
under boards or through cracks, and we went to bed in
cold rooms with cold feet.

Except the hall, we had only a kitchen and bedrooms
in our house. We used one of the bedrooms as the main
setting room. It had a big fireplace and one rocking
chair. Pa or Grandma usually set in it. Ma kept her
quilting frame in the room with the fireplace. She rolled
it up to the ceiling when she wasn't quilting. They was
a bureau with a looking glass in one corner near the
fireplace. Pa and Rufe shaved at the bureau on Sunday
morning when it was too cold to shave at the shelf washstand on the back porch. The old Cherokee single-bar-
reled shotgun hung in a rack over one of the doors.
Ma's broomstraw broom stood near a pile of wood for
the fire. In the morning me and Rufe brought in enough

wood to last for the day, and at night we piled up enough to last until bedtime and to start a fire the next morning.

In the main setting room Ma put up two little red cards with gold letters on them. They said "God Bless Our Home" and "Fear Not Little Flock." We kept calendars nailed on the wall. You could tell from them when to plant crops and kill hogs and what the weather was going to be. They advertised tonics and medicines like Wine of Cardui and Lydia E. Pinkham's Vegetable Compound. Dr. Ramon's Liver Pills showed a doctor with a black long-tailed coat and a big flat-topped hat; he carried a black medicine case in one hand and a walking stick in the other. Every home had a calendar advertising Black Draught. Wiley Cochran said Black Draught was made out of the devil's snuff. It tasted so bad, he said, a feller's system couldn't stand it. It went through him so fast he'd have to start running for the woods before he'd drunk it all down.

We always needed one or two more chairs. When one of us children went to the kitchen for something to eat, another one got his chair. We kept a pot of cottonseed hanging over the fire in the winter and biling so they'd be soft enough for the cows to eat. We set around close to the fire at night and burned our legs while our backs was chilly. If one of us stood close to the fire to get warm, he kept the heat from reaching the rest of us, and we fussed till he set down. The hot fire baked the blood in the front of the girls' legs, and they looked bloodshotten or piedidy. My older sisters wore thick cotton stockings and kept their dresses pulled down low for protection from the fire, but every woman had piedidy legs until the middle of summer.

We popped popcorn and cracked and et walnuts and hickornuts. We just had one corn popper, and it took a long time to pop enough for Pa, Ma, Grandma, and us ten children. Some of us worked by the light of the fire and a kerosene lamp. The biggest boys helped Pa make fishbaskets and cotton-picking baskets out of splits from white oak trees, sharpened our knives, made bird traps, cleaned our guns, melted lead and molded bullets for the hog rifles, reloaded old shotgun shells, visited with neighbors, told stories, and talked about kinfolks and farming. Sometimes we just set and looked at the fire. Ma said she could see visions in the red embers and the flames. We felt comfortable when the wind howled through the tops of the pines and around the corners of the house and through the hall. The last one going to bed kivered the fire. He shoveled ashes on it so Pa could build a fire quick the next morning.

Pa paid Old Uncle Allen, a white-bearded colored man in Ball Ground, twenty-five cents a chair to weave new chair bottoms of white-oak splits. He brought white-oak posts, six feet long and four inches square. First with a froe and then with a knife he made splits about a half-inch wide and the thickness of cardboard. Uncle Allen always et dinner at the home where he bottomed chairs. Us children had heard tales that no colored man ever sneezed, but Uncle Allen often pulled a little splinter from one of the splits and tickled his nose and made hisself sneeze. He told jokes and stories about haints, graveyards, mysterious things, and strange deaths.

In every other room in the house except the hall and the kitchen we had at least two beds. Some families put four beds in a room, one in each corner. Ma and the girls quilted off and on all winter long, and nearly everybody had more quilts than they could use. Nobody ever got cold for lack of cover, but it's a wonder why no child ever got mashed to death sleeping under eight or ten quilts. Most folks thought a lot of cover was mighty comfortable on a cold night, but Rufe said so many quilts made him feel like he'd been run through the surp cane mill. Ma kept ducks and geese and plucked the feathers for featherbeds and pillows. We didn't have bedspreads and mattresses. A straw tick made a good mattress. When we first stuffed wheat or oat straw into a new tick it was three feet high. Going to bed was like climbing a haystack. The little fellers had to have a chair to crawl up on the beds. The baby slept in a homemade cradle, a box with long rockers under each end. When Ma set down to work, she set near the cradle and rocked it with her foot. If the baby cried while she was moving about in her work, one of us children rocked the cradle.

Pa didn't build closets in the bedrooms. We hung our few clothes in a chifforobe or on nails behind the door, and we kept our shoes under the bed. When Pa and Ma had so many children that they run out of bedrooms and beds, we built another room on the side of the house. We put walls around one end of the front porch and tacked another room on the back porch the same way. If a winder pane broke, Ma stuck a feather pillow in the hole to keep out the cold and the rain. When money was scarce, that pillow stayed in the hole all winter.

Many times we was bothered by bedbugs or chinches. They come to our house with visiting neighbors. It was common for folks to have bedbugs, but a disgrace to keep them. Some people just got used to the bugs and let them bite and never tried to get shed of them. Ma hated bedbugs. She filled fruitjar lids with lamp oil and set the bedposts in the lids. Then the bugs could not jump or swim across the lamp oil to the bed. To get shed of the bugs, she biled water, tore down the bedsteads, scalded the bedbugs to death with water and lye soap, washed the quilts, scalded the featherbeds, sunned the beds, poured biling water on every slat, sloshed scalding water on the walls and in all the cracks between the planks. Sometimes she scrubbed and washed and sloshed with turpentine or lamp oil. She picked the bedbugs off the strawticks and used hairpins to gouge them out of crevices in the bed and the floor. Some bugs hid deep in cracks, and neighbors always brought more. After all the scalding and scrubbing there was nearly always some chinches left to breed a new generation.

The kitchen was next to Pa and Ma's bedroom. It had a table, chairs, a coffee grinder, a stove, a pile of stove-wood, and a bin for corn meal and flour. In the corner was a big bucket of scraps and slop for the hogs. In the coldest part of winter we kept a bucket of water and a dipper and a washpan on a washstand in the kitchen. We hung a flour sack or a guanner sack on a nail on the door and used it for a towel. Ma's stove was a little square metal box of a thing without even a warming closet. All the old stoves was made too short. Pa put a big box about ten inches high under the stove so Ma wouldn't have to stoop.

Pa built our kitchen table out of pine boards, and he took time to taper the legs. I remember a pretty oilcloth Ma had, yellow with red roses and green leaves. Every child had a regular place to eat. The boys set on a home-made bench between the table and the wall, and the girls set in chairs on the opposite side of the table. Ma and Pa et at the ends of the table. Hungry boys reached all the way across the table for a platter of food. Us boys used to laugh at a story about a good-sized boy that still wore a little boy's apron. One time he reached across the table for some surp, and his Pa said, "Ma, you better sew that boy some breeches. Did you see what he drug through the gravy?"

For a long time we didn't have screens or fly swatters, and folks had to get along with flies the best they could. Most folks didn't know that flies was nasty, and they wasn't bothered when flies walked about on their food. When we et, Ma or Lucy scared off the flies with a fan or peacock tail feathers or a branch of a tree. A few flies still lit on the food. When we was done eating, Ma kivered the table with a big tablecloth to keep flies off the left-overs. When I was a little boy I shore did despise to eat meals with some of our neighbors. Oncet I et dinner with a neighbor family, and nobody minded the flies off the table while they et. They just swarmed all over everything. I had to force-feed myself every bite I et.

A long narrow back porch run all the way across the back of the house. The well was at one end and a shelf for a waterbucket, a dipper, and a tin washpan. We liked a cedar bucket because a metal bucket gives the water a bad taste. Even on the coldest days when us children washed our hands and faces in the kitchen, Pa always washed outside. Sometimes in the early morning on a cold day he had to break the ice off the top of the water bucket before he washed his face in the icy water.

I never heard of an inside bathroom until I was grown, and only a few folks used chamberpots or slop jars. Some of our neighbors didn't even build outdoor toilets; they just used a certain place in the woods, and you could always tell where it was by the corn cobs. One time Gay Wheeler broke his leg while he was logging at the sawmill. He couldn't squat down in the woods; so he had his folks to nail up a board between two trees, and he held on to it and sorta hunkered over and stuck his bad leg out to the side. Then a terrible rising come on his nose. It was big and red as a bloody beet. The broke leg and a sore nose was about as much as any one feller could stand, but poor old Gay got a miserable belly ache on one of the coldest nights I ever saw in my life. He had et a big bait of crackling bread, and it give him the scours and diarrhea. Five times that night he had to get out of his warm bed and go out in the cold and hold on to his board and hunker over while the wind whistled around his tail.

All winter long us children shoveled ashes from the stove and the fireplace, toted them out to the ash hopper in the back yard, and kivered them with boards to keep them dry. In the spring Ma showed us how to make lye. Early in the morning we begun pouring water in the ashes. It took nearly all day for it to get started to dripping. The water dropped out into a trough or a pot or pitcher. Then Ma took grease, old leftover bones, gristle, and strong meat and put them in the lye made from the ashes and biled that nearly all day. When it cooled, we had lye soap. That's what we washed our hands with. It took the dirt off and sometimes a little skin with it. Ma and the girls washed floors and clothes with the soap. Me and Rufe even washed the dogs with it, and it killed all the fleas. Sometimes the hogs got lice and run under the house. We'd take soapy water and splosh up under the house to kill the lice.

We mopped the house with sand and lye soap and homemade mops. Pa made mops by boring holes about an inch apart in a board twelve to eighteen inches long. Then we stuffed the inside white of the shuck of an ear of corn through the hole until it was tight. Then Pa put a handle on the piece of wood, and the spring mopping begun.

If the weather was good, washdays was fun for the little children. But washing clothes was pretty bad work in the winter. On Monday morning we packed the clothes in the tubs and carried them a quarter of a mile to the spring on a sled or in a old wore-out buggy. A trough from the spring carried water to the tubs and the washpot. We built a fire under one side of the pot and biled some of the clothes in water and lye soap. On a windy day when the wind shifted a whole lot, the smoke caused tears and red eyes. Ever oncet in a while Ma took some of the clothes out of the pot and beat them on the wash bench with a battling stick. It always took us a good half a day to wash the clothes. We rubbed and jobbed and rubbed and biled and stirred and beat. Beuler Jordan was the best hand with a battling stick in the settlement. She lived a half a mile from our house, and we'd hear her battling her clothes every washday. Ma'd say, "Beuler shore is making the buttons fly like hot popcorn. Looks like she'd remember how much sewing she's gonna have to do."

We did not own an ice box or an electric refrigerator. Ma put the milk and butter in lard buckets and kept them cool in a spring some distance from the house. When a cloudburst or a waterspout come, us children had to dash out and bring the milk to the house. Sometimes the milk and butter washed away down the branch. Some folks who didn't have a spring kept their milk in an earthenware jar in a storm cellar. Others put the milk in a long tin pail and lowered it into the well. It had to be lowered mighty careful. If it sunk too deep, water seeped under the lid and into the milk.

In the old days a man had to make just about everything he had. Most young couples started life with two beds, a stove, a wardrobe, a table, and a little mirror. They could furnish a home for thirty-five dollars. Sometimes in a cold house they had to paste newspaper or brown wrapping paper on the walls and the ceiling. When the wind blowed, the ceiling rattled. Sometimes a feller couldn't afford sawed boards, and he used an adze to split four-inch planks from a pine log. He made puncheon floors, and they was mighty rough. The baby's high chair was made out of the crooked limbs and roots of the winter huckleberry bush. Women plaited old pieces of cloth and sewed them together for homemade rugs.

The farmer growed his own food and made his own clothes. Salt and coffee was the main groceries Pa had to buy, and some folks even did without coffee. When we didn't have sugar, we used sorghum surp. We took in anywhere from twenty-five to two hundred dollars a year on the farm, and Pa tried not to spend more than ten or twenty dollars a year for groceries.

Breakfast was our main meal. Ma's biscuits was as big as Pa's fist, and Ma thought us boys was puny if we couldn't eat at least six. We et our meats for breakfast—

chicken, steak, fish, salmon, ham, fresh pork, sausage, sidemeat, rabbit parebiled and then fried, quail, and squirrel. Ma cooked all the meats until they was mighty well done, and she breaded all of them in meal or flour except salmon and hog meat. Ma shore could make good gravy for us to sop our biscuits in—thickening gravy and hogeye or redeye or ham gravy. Surp mixed with ham gravy was mighty good. Pa raised wheat for the biscuits and had the flour ground at Moore's water mill on Shoal Creek. Sunday was the day for big meals and big eating. In lean years we lived on cornbread all week, but feasted on biscuits on Sunday morning.

Pa bought green coffee beans from the store, Ma parched them over the stove in a skillet, and my sister Frony ground them in a little hand-turned coffee mill nailed to the wall. Not many folks could afford ready-ground coffee. A few times Pa bought a sack of strong black Arbuckle coffee. It always had one striped stick of peppermint candy in the package. We never did buy a percolator; Ma biled the coffee in her old black iron kittle, and she poured a little cold water in it when it biled to make the grounds settle to the bottom. Us children poured our coffee out in a saucer and blowed on it to cool it. We drunk coffee when we was a baby; Ma crumbled a little piece of biscuit in sweetened coffee and fed it to the baby. Some poor folks that couldn't buy coffee toasted cornmeal over the fire until it burned almost black. When it was biled in a black kittle, folks said it tasted a little bit like coffee.

For dinner and supper we et cornbread and vegetables cooked with sidemeat or fatback. What few meats we et for dinner or supper was always biled. Ma made cobblers and flat pies and tarts out of dried or canned fruit. She sweetened the pies with surp, and we et all kinds of pies—blackberry, dewberry, huckleberry, wild and tame strawberry, apple, peach, and plum. The hulls of the muscadine made a good strong-tasting pie. Old Doc

Hawkins told Pa that the seed of blackberries, dewberries, and strawberries clogged up the appendix and caused appendicitis. Ma was afraid for us to eat berries for a while. But old Pete Jordan, a colored man, changed her mind. He said, "Wild berries and possums and rabbits was made by the good Lawd for niggers and pore white folks."

Nearly everybody had enough to eat, but many times they wasn't much change in the victuals. Sometimes folks had to fill up on just what they could find. Grandma was always pleased when sweet potater time come. Then she knowed that the Purks children had plenty to eat. Sweet potater time was their fattening season. Sly Suggs had a hard time feeding his family. "Take a little bite of meat, son," he'd say, "and a big bite of bread." One time I went possum hunting with a colored boy, Oscar Kellog. I got to Oscar's house before the family et supper, and I heard his Pa call out, "Oscar, you know you ain't worked any today. Don't eat much."

One time Webb Roberts hired poor old Abe Purks to sprout a new ground for him. Webb had a curiosity to know what Abe brought for dinner, and he slipped and looked in Abe's lard-can dinner bucket. Abe'd hung it up on a limb in a tree to keep it away from the dogs. They wasn't nothing but a pone of cornbread in it. After that, Webb always took Abe a jar of milk or a plate of pie or something like that. Webb told Pa he was ashamed of his curiosity, but Abe had a big family to feed, and Webb wanted to help him as much as he could.

We et a lot of wild foods. Me and Rufe fished and caught fish in baskets and et eels and turkles and gigged bullfrogs and et the legs. We shot squirrels and rabbits and caught them in traps and boxes and killed birds with deadfalls. We picked wild berries and foxgrapes and muscadines, and gathered hickornuts, walnuts, chestnuts, and chinkypins. A lot of greens grew wild: swamp cresses and wild lettuce and poke salet in the spring before the pokeweed got old and poisonous. Ma made persimmon beer. She mixed persimmons and apple cores and peelings in a barrel and added a layer of wheat straw to make it settle and strain out the trash. Sometimes she put in sweet potaters and pods from locust trees. We drunk a lot of persimmon beer when the cow went dry. Pa kept beehives back of the smokehouse, and Luke learnt how to follow a wild bee to a tree full of honey. In the bees' working season he went to a branch and watched the bees coming in to the edge of the water. Then the bee flew in a straight bee line to the hive.

Most folks raised a lot of kinds of meat: hogs, cattle, sheep, and goats. When they killed an animal, they et just about every bit of it. Hog-killing days was a time of plenty. What couldn't be salted down had to be et quick before it spiled. We liked hog feet and ears and brains and kidneys and hearts and liver and lights and jowls and even the tail. Ma fried the grease out of the fattest meat and the entrails, and she ground up the cracklings and cooked them in cornbread. And chitlins. Us boys carried the entrails to the wash place. Ma split and cleaned them, turned them inside out, washed them, put them in a tub, washed them with homemade lye soap, and placed them under a spout of water that come from the spring. They soaked for several days. Then Ma and the girls plaited the small ones, just like a plait in a child's hair. Ma fried them and the rest of the chitlins and the stomach, or punch. Matt Price sure did love chitlins. He said he could eat a gut as long as from here to Marietta and a punch at every station.

We was always anxious for a new crop to come in so we could have a change. Before the new corn was dry enough to harvest, the old got full of weevils and soiled by rats. Before the earliest corn was fully dried out on the stalk, we gathered some of it, shelled it, and spread it out to dry on a sheet on the roof of the smokehouse. New corn made good cornbread at about the same time the first sorghum surp come in. New cornbread and new surp with butter and milk was mighty good.

All of us took pride in putting up food for the winter. It was hard to get money to buy glass Mason jars, lids, and rubbers. We stored surp in metal cans, glass jars, clay jugs, and wooden barrels. We took a big sewing needle and strung bean pods on strings about a yard long and hung them on the porch until they was dry. Then we pulled the beans, or leather breeches, off the strings and stored them in flour sacks. They was dry and brittle as shucks. Leather breeches had to soak for hours before they was cooked. Us children could smell cooking leather breeches as soon as we opened the front door when we come home from school, and we run for the big black pot and beans to eat between meals. Biled with a piece of sidemeat, the beans was good, but they always had a dry burned taste.

In the fall we cut round circles from punkins and dried them. They shriveled up like a busted balloon and had to be soaked a long time before they was cooked. Stewed pumpkin was strong-tasting and pulpy. Beans, peas, sweet potaters, and Arsh potaters did not have to be canned or dried. Ma and the girls picked beans, apples, and peaches. We chopped up cabbages and made a fifty-gallon barrel of kraut. Grandma made us keep the kraut and pickled beans down in the cellar on a piece of marble. She said that kept them from getting too old and sour. We raised a big crop of beans, and we et dried beans all winter. Ma didn't have bottles for the babies, and she fed the baby beansoup. Many times she chewed up the food for the baby and put the soft pap in its mouth.

We liked cold cornbread and milk for supper. On a rainy and snowy day while we was setting around the fire, Ma'd say, "How'd you like a pot of mush?"

"OOOoohhh," we'd say, "we'd like it."

Mush, cornmeal biled in salt and water, was a change.

Pa said, "Always remember, children, in eating mush, dip your spoon in the milk first and then eat your mush because then the mush won't stick to the spoon." All of us dipped our spoons in the same pot. During the night the left-over mush hardened, and the next morning Ma sliced it and fried it in hot grease. Fried mush, surp, and coffee made a good breakfast. Pa said a mush breakfast gave a man strength for a good day's work.

Our clothes was homemade just like our victuals. We had to do without, to make the best use of what we had, and to find new uses for old rags and clothes. Late in the fall each child got one pair of shoes to last all winter. If we wore our shoes out before spring, we had to go barefoot or borrow shoes from a brother or sister when we went outdoors. Each year Pa bought two or three pairs of overhalls, and about every ten years he bought a new blue-serge suit. When the breeches wore out, he bought a new pair of pants to go with the coat. A feller in the country didn't need a suit often. When he went visiting on Sunday he wore his best overhalls and a clean homemade blue shirt. Once a month the church held service, and Pa greased his work shoes and put on his Sunday suit. He never wore a tie.

Not many men had a good everyday work coat. A wore-out Sunday blue-serge suit might do for a work coat for a little while. Some people wore blue denim jackets. Many a man didn't have a coat; he just wore a vest and enough underwear and shirts to keep warm. Everybody wore long-handled winter underwear. World War I provided many a man with an army overcoat, a short coat, and breeches. They was warm, and you just couldn't wear them out. Most men liked the army color, but a few dyed their army clothes black and changed the buttons.

None of the girls ever owned a store-bought dress. Their underwear was homemade. Some women wore a lot of petticoats with wide red bands sewed on the bottom. They spun thread and knitted stockings. A woman who had no sewing machine visited a neighbor to sew or did all her sewing with a needle and thread. Luraline Worsham made herself a bustle and stuffed it with sawdust. Hubert Holbert hit her with the ball during a game of town ball, and sawdust just flew all over the place. Hubert hollered, "Luraline, your bustle is a-leaking its stuffing," and she throwed it in the bushes and said she'd just have to make out without it.

We never did have much money. All of us worked, but we just barely made a living. After Pa paid his taxes, he started saving nickels and dimes to be ready to pay his county taxes the next year. The tax collector wouldn't take calves and chickens and eggs and hogs. Sometimes Pa hired out as a day laborer at fifty cents to a dollar a day when he wasn't working in the field. He split cordwood or worked at a sawmill for fifty cents a day. Jasper Hendrix traveled all over the settlement cutting wheat with a cradle for a dollar a day. He demanded top wages because of his skill and the hard work it took to cut wheat. For binding wheat, a man was paid seventy-five cents a day, and a woman bound wheat all day long for fifty cents. Bill Farmer grew corn, took it to a water mill two miles from his home, paid the miller one-eighth as toll, then hauled the meal to the marble quarry at Marble Hill ten miles away, and sold three bushels for a dollar.

Our pleasures was homemade. A man rolled his own cigarettes, and even then they was too expensive except for weekends and special times. For a nickel a man could buy a big yellow package of Victory tobacco. I remember the cloth tobacco sacks had drawstrings and a picture of an Indian on them. The tobacco was packed so tight that they was enough in the sack to fill a quart bucket. When the sacks was empty, boys used them to hold their marbles or tin tobacco tags from plug chewing tobacco. Old people raised tobacco on a little patch of new ground. They twisted chewing tobacco into lengths about ten inches long, big in the middle and tapering gradually to a point at each end.

Most pipes was cob pipes. Aunt Clary Thomas smoked a clay pipe with a long slender cane stem. Her husband run away a few months after they was married. She visited us a whole lot. She'd set at the fireplace, crumble her tobacco from her apron pocket, pack it into her pipe, lay a live coal from the fire on top of the tobacco, and then puff on the pipe. She didn't have any teeth. When she sucked on the pipe, her mouth looked like the blossom end of a swiveled cucumber. When she took the pipe stem out of her mouth, it left a little hole just the size of the pipe stem. She'd look mighty content when she blowed a stream of smoke through that little opening in her mouth.

Most tobacco chewers toted a twist of homemade tobacco and a piece of a plug from the store, usually Brown Mule. Mixed home-grown and store-bought tobacco was a good cheap chew. Bought plugs had a surp in the tobacco, and sometimes Pa bought some of the surp and mixed it with his home-grown tobacco. Star tobacco was thick and waxy; it was the best store-bought tobacco. It caused a feller to spit a lot, and the ambeer was the color of ham gravy. If a feller had a plug of Star his friends would say, "Give me a chew of the Star so's I can chew Star Navy and spit ham gravy."

Tobacco-chewers and snuff-dippers was proud of the way they could spit. Frank Patton could put some kind of pressure behind his load of ambeer and knock the eyes out of a toad-frog ten feet away. Oscar Jordan just squirted the juice out like a goose that has been eating grass; part of it went on his shirt, and some of it oozed out of the corners of his mouth and dripped off. My brother Rufe could open his lips, keep his teeth closed, and squirt a small stream between the teeth. Women that dipped snuff was neater spitters than men.

A lot of men wore untrimmed mustaches, and the tobacco juice made the hairs close to the mouth look like little threads of old gold. Charley Bell's long mustache was black, gray, gold, and all sorts of colors.

I never owned a store-bought toy. We made our own little wagons with wooden wheels and dogwood axles. Round blocks from a blackgum or a sweetgum tree made good wheels. We couldn't tell which way a tree would fall when we cut it down, and we was scared it would fall on us. After we had cut halfway through the trunk, we would saw a little and run, slip back up to the tree, saw a little more and run. Pa didn't own a brace and bit; so we heated an iron rod red-hot and burned a hole through the wheels for the axle. If we didn't have axle grease for the wooden wheels, we used lard. On a steep hill them homemade wagons would run mighty fast. We made sleds and rode them downhill on slick pine needles and tried to dodge the pine trees.

Us children always enjoyed playing. It was a lot of fun just not to have to work. We knowed how to make many toys. A good strong flip would kill a rabbit if you could shoot it straight. We pushed the pith out of a length of elder wood, used a piece of broomstraw as a dart, made a trigger with a rubber band, and used the gun to kill flies. Elders or large canes from the canebrake made good popguns and squirtguns. Chewed up paper or little chunks of potater was good wadding. A piece of potater from a popgun could raise a blister when it hit bare skin. Water guns made of elder or cane would squirt a stream of water thirty feet.

Even when a man could not make what he needed at home, somebody in the settlement made it for him. The blacksmith, Alf Ridings, could make just about any tool needed on the farm. For a long time I wanted to be a blacksmith when I growed up. I enjoyed turning the big old fan that was the bellows. Plows glowed red and white hot, the hammer clanged on the anvil, and the tempered

metal smelled clean and sour. Alf's hands was so calloused and horny that he could pick up the hot eye of
a stove with his bare hand. When he sharpened a plow,
he trimmed off red-hot curls of metal from the edge. One
time when little Clyde Ridings was running around his
pa's shop he stepped on one of the hot curls and stood
on it. Alf smelled something like burning horn and said,
"Clyde, if you keep on a-standing on that hot ahrn, it's
gonna burn through them calluses on your feet atter a
while. If you won't look where you walk in the shop,
I'll just have to make you some mule shoes and nail
em on."

Alf sharpened a plow for fifteen cents. For $1.50 he
welded a new blade on an old ax which had been
sharpened so many times that the blade was nearly
ground off. He made and sold cradles for cutting wheat.
He built homemade wagons and wagon wheels and axles.

Many folks owned homemade tar-grinding wagons. The
axle turned in a box filled with damp tar instead of
grease. When the tar dried out, it was nearly as hard as
iron, and the wheel locked. On long trips a man had to
stop to wet the tar or to buy new tar. In dry weather,
wooden wheels of wagons shrunk up and nearly fell to
pieces. Then you had to stop and water the wheel so it
would stay together and hold the tire on. Sometimes
a man drove wedges under the steel tires to hold them
on. A wagon with wedges all around the four wheels
looked mighty strange. When a horse or a mule had a
hard time pulling a heavy load up a steep hill, a man
walked on the spokes of the wheels to help the team.

Most of the shoes and boots wore in the hill country
was homemade. Old Josh Moody was the best shoe-
maker in our settlement. He raised cows, slaughtered
them, skinned them, and tanned the hides. He hired
men to cut tanning bark off mountain oaks and white
oaks. After the bark dried, Josh ground it up in a mill
and put it in vats with water. He soaked hides in the

54

ooze to loosen the hair and cure the skin. Shoes, saddles, harness, and bridles—Josh could make anything out of leather. Homemade boots and shoes was mighty stiff. When they got old they was fairly comfortable, but it was hard to break a new pair in. Rough new shoes peeled the skin off a boy's feet. He'd wear the shoes a day or two, and then go barefooted again until his feet got well. Then he put on the shoes and wore the hide off his feet again.

Old Joe Starnes and one-armed Joe Watkins built the homemade coffins. They charged just a few dollars, and when the neighbors couldn't pay, they made a coffin for nothing and sometimes even furnished the materials. A few coffins was made out of just raw, unpainted, unplaned boards. Sometimes they painted a coffin. The best ones was covered with velvet, and Joe Starnes even learned to curve the sides. Nearly always the inside was lined with cloth, anything from cheesecloth to silk. Some of the women sewed a little satin pillow.

Old man Marn Jackson made his living by trapping on Sharp Mountain Creek and the Etowah River. He knowed the habits of minks and muskrats. When we gathered corn in the river bottom on cold November days we could hear Old Marn splashing around and running his muskrat traps. One time I stole a mighty dead possum from one of his traps, skinned it, and sold the hide for forty cents. That possum worried me for many a day.

Hardship families in the old days didn't get welfare checks from the government. A few poor widows received five or ten dollars a month from the county. Poor folks lived a hard life and did the best they could. Sometimes when they run plumb out of food they stole a sack of corn from the crib, a piece of meat from the smokehouse, or a couple of chickens from the henhouse. Not many farmers padlocked their corn cribs and smokehouses. Pa tried to keep an old dog for a guard. Most old dogs was mean and suspicious at night. Old Lead slept in the shuck house and he barked and growled fierce enough to scare away prowlers.

One time Pa thought corn was disappearing from the crib, and he set a bear trap and caught Lum Latimer by the hand. Lum screamed and called for help for a while, and then Pa let him loose and asked him to come on back to the house with him and eat breakfast with us. Lum promised Pa he'd never steal again.

The Hopkinses stole corn a lot of times, but they was so needy that nobody wanted to catch them. When they stole something from Pa, he said he guessed it was his turn to make a donation to charity.

Folks that look back at the old times now think it was a hard life, but then it was just the way of living. Most folks thought they was doing pretty well. Calvin Farmer worked hard all his life, and he told Pa he didn't have any regrets. "I've always tried to be on a average," Calvin says. "I don't want to be up high, and I don't want to be down dragging. I want to be medium. I had plenty to eat, sich as it was. And I didn't know that other people had more. When people got old, their family tuck care of them. Widders especially worked hard, and some of them lived hard too. Many a woman had to plow, and at times they had mighty pore eating. But the pore farmer stuck it out, and he didn't know his life was as hard as it was."

THE HOLCOMBS AND THE MOSSES

To "keep the sifter going," Jim Holcomb and his sons had to work all the time. During winter and between the laying-by of the crops and fodder-pulling time, Jim worked as a section hand on the railroad ten hours a day for ninety cents. During moving time in the fall he and his neighbor Gordon Covington moved families in their two-horse wagons from one farm to another.

The Holcombs cultivated about twenty acres of cotton and twenty of corn. They tended patches of syrup cane, potatoes, turnips, beans, peas, and a little wheat. Always there was work to be done: water to tote from the well about fifty yards from the house, wood to cut and haul for the huge fireplace, stovewood to be cut, stock to be fed, and food to cook.

Besides Jim and his wife and their ten children, Mrs. Holcomb's mother and father, Frank Moss and his wife, lived in the little four-room house across the railroad from Sharp Mountain Church. "Cowline" (Caroline) Moss was sixteen years older than her husband. Frank had the merriest heart in the settlement. He fished and hunted a great deal with teen-age boys. He was proud of his Cherokee shotgun with shiny metal around the breech, the fanciest gun in the community. After everyone else changed to smokeless powder, Frank still used the old black-powder shells. After he shot he had to wait a moment before the smoke cleared enough for him to tell whether he had killed anything.

Because of a club foot and a bad limp, Frank could not plow, but he took pride in being a good cotton chopper, fodder puller, and woodcutter. When Frank bought a new ax, Led Lee asked him the name brand. To keep his friend from knowing that he could not read, Frank handed Led the ax and said, "My eyes is bad. You read it."

Between the laying-by of the crops in July and fodder-pulling time, he gathered peaches for ten cents an hour or a dollar a day. He cut firewood or cordwood for seventy-five cents a day. Jim Holcomb furnished his groceries. All he bought was his clothing, two pairs of shoes a year, two pairs of overalls, and every ten years a pair of Sunday pants and a coat. His dollar-and-a-half watch wore out about every two years, and his wife gave him another one.

Not many passers-by walked the lonely road by the Holcomb farm. When someone did come near, Frank's big black hound raised a loud alarm. Lurey and Lillie

Mae kept the clay yard swept clean with a brush broom. After Lurey finished churning, she set the churn out in the yard to sun. Once Hu Watkins's enormous hound, Pup, smelled and sniffed around Lurey's churn. Then he turned his back to the churn, raised as high as he could on his hind legs, and made a deposit right in the churn. No other dog could have reached so high. Hu always wondered what Lurey thought happened to her churn, but he never dared ask.

One of Jim's boys, Clarice, had attended a business college in Atlanta. He took a job working for Sam Tate, Road Commissioner of the state and President of the Georgia Marble Company in Tate, six miles away. During World War I, Mr. Tate talked the Holcomb boy into volunteering to join the army. In New York, Clarice took pneumonia. One night at eleven o'clock his mother, knowing he had pneumonia, said, "My son is dying at eleven o'clock." The next day the Holcomb family received a telegram saying, "Your son died at eleven o'clock last night." He was the first soldier buried in Sharp Mountain Cemetery since the Civil War.

4

Field Work

(As Remembered and Told by Jess Hudgins)

When we was working the crop in the spring and summer, Pa jumped out of bed just at break of day. He slept in his underwear or the shirt he worked in the day before if he hadn't sweated in it too much. He put on his breeches and brogan shoes without socks and went to the barn to feed the mules and hogs while Ma cooked breakfast. Pa said that smelling the home-cured meat frying in the kitchen while he went back and forth from the barn to the hog lot made him mighty hungry.

Pa liked to get up early and see the sunrise and the dew. He loved his mules, cattle, and hogs. The world, he said, seemed like a good place in the early morning. But us children wasn't pleased with the early rising. The signal for us to get up was the grinding of the old-fashioned coffee mill. After the coffee was ground, they was just enough time to get up, put on clothes, wash, and be ready for breakfast. Rufe had to be fussed out of bed every morning. Sometimes he lifted his leg, rolled over, stomped on the floor to show that he was out of bed, and went back to sleep. But Pa didn't put up with that trick many times.

Frony helped Ma cook breakfast, and Lucy fixed the dinner to take to the fields. She went to the garden and pulled up bunches of green onions or shallots to take to the field, and she left the peelings on them to keep them fresh until dinner. We saved the shoulder meat of a hog to make a crop on. Lucy packed cornbread and biscuits and meat and a vegetable in the dinner basket, and an extra hunk of cornbread for an evening between-meal and for the dogs that went with us to the field. The spring near the field wasn't always clean, and Lucy filled a jug of water and one of buttermilk. Me and Rufe packed corn and fodder in the wagon for the mules.

Just after Pa et he said, "Well, let's git to work," and him and me and Rufe went to the barn. We spent ten or fifteen minutes brushing the salty sweat off the mule with a currycomb and a brush. Sometimes when we didn't have a currycomb or a brush we used a fresh corncob. We cleaned the sweat from the collar with a towsack; then Pa checked the shoulders of the mule to see that the collar hadn't caused sores. Pa said a man oughter take better care of his mules than he did hisself.

Pa and Rufe rode the two mules; and the hoe-hands, the girls and us younger boys, walked. We didn't take the wagon to the field except when we worked in the far field and took our dinner or when we carried seed or fertilizer or tools. Even fat mules had backbones as sharp as a razor, and sometimes Pa let me ride when his tail was sore because of corncobs or galded with sweat. Sometimes Pa rode sideways.

When we got to the field, we sharpened the hoes while Lucy hung the big dinner basket on a tree in the shade so the ants and the dogs couldn't reach it. Just before he started plowing, Pa usually had something to say to Rufe. "Rufe, yesterday you didn't kiver up enough of the little grass. You know that saves lots of hoeing. The children are gitting behind with their hoeing, and we need to help them with the plow as much as we can. And watch old Kate and don't let her break down any of the cornstalks at the end of the row."

Our neighbor across the river, General Wheeler, prided

hisself on being the earliest riser in the settlement. He got to the field so early in the morning that he had to wait until it was light enough for him to see how to plow. One time Pa vowed to beat old man Wheeler to the field at least one time. While Pa was leaning on his plowstock, waiting a minute for enough light to plow his young corn, he heard old man Wheeler holler, "Gee!"

Fresh plowed earth in the morning smells and feels like nothing else in this world. A man busting up a field in the spring feels like he's doing something nobody ever done before. Ground where brushpiles and trash have burned has mighty sharp smells, specially in the early morning when the ground is fresh with dew.

We worked till about nine o'clock and then stopped to git a drink of water. Then we plowed and hoed till dinner time. Then we et and rested an hour. Rufe and Pa laid down and slept, and some of the children played. Then we worked till the sun went down. Pa didn't have a watch. The evening seemed like it never would end; the least children kept asking how long it was till quitting time. Pa'd stretch his arm full length toward the sun and hold his four fingers close together between his eyes and the sun. Each hand width between the sun and its setting place meant an hour before the setting of the sun and the end of the day's work. Just at dark we drug ourselves home. By the time Pa had freed the mules in the barn, General Wheeler had done gone to bed, resting up to be first in the field the next day.

May and June was the months of back-breaking field work. All the children six years and over had to chop cotton and hoe the weeds out of the corn and the other crops. We usually hoed corn three times in a season, and cotton more often. If they was a long rainy spell, we had to hoe the cotton until it bloomed in July.

My sisters wore bonnets with wide brims and stockings on their arms and hands to keep off the sunshine. White skin rather than suntans was the style. A girl had to hoe until she married, and even then women had to hoe except when they was pregnant. A lot of times Ma took the baby to the fields and left it on a pallet under a tree while she hoed.

Becoming a plow hand was a big step in getting to be a man. Pa thought all us boys would be a farmer just like he was, and he taught us how to farm and to work while we was young. A boy was supposed to work and to stay at home until he was twenty-one years old. Then he was free to marry, leave home, and work for hisself.

Most folks was as good to their children as they had a chance to be, but some mighty sad things happened in some families. George Mullinax and his family of twelve children lived on a farm that was so poor that it wouldn't hardly sprout peas. They barely managed to get something to eat and wear. One time a cheap carnival come to town, and George promised to take his children to the show if they finished all the work he told them to do. They worked fast and chopped a mighty lot of cotton, but George begun to worry about the money. While them poor wore-out children was riding home from the fields in the wagon, George told them that he'd had to change his mind because of the money. He went to the show by hisself, but he promised to tell them all about it when he got back.

The hard field work begun in the spring when we got the land ready for the crops. We chopped down dead cornstalks and cottonstalks, piled them up, and burnt them on spots where they was a heavy growth of crabgrass. Then Pa and Rufe plowed the field with a turning plow, broke up the clods with a harrow, and laid off the rows for the crops. Me and Lucy and Frony rolled the cottonseed in water and ashes to keep them from clinging together in wads. The planter was a long horn made of tin with a funnel on one end. Us children planted the seed while Pa and Rufe laid off the rows and kivered the seed. We carried buckets of seed corn and dropped one grain at each step and one in between. In the rich soil of the creek bottom, we planted twicet as much corn as we did in the poor soil of the hills. As we dropped the seed, we spread guanner in the rows. Fertilizer always came in two-hundred-pound bags, and Angie Evans said that every farmer ought to use Lion brand guanner because it stunk more. You could see fishbones and flesh in Lion guanner and know it had plant food in it. Pa used Red Steer guanner, which didn't smell as bad as the Lion. A feller who didn't use exactly two hundred pounds of fertilizer to the acre was considered a man of poor judgment.

We cultivated about fifteen acres of cotton and corn for each mule, but sometimes when many children was at home Pa planted as much as twenty acres per animal. Pa and Ma made about two bales of cotton the first few years they was married. When me and Rufe got big enough to work, Pa made about three bales. Later on when Rufe could plow and several children was big enough to work Pa kept two mules and made six or eight bales. We never did make a bale to the acre. We growed enough corn for bread and feed for the stock. Pa owned a little rich bottom land and we didn't need to plant as much corn as an upland farmer.

Farmers didn't build terraces and lay out the rows in contour with the land, and rows sometimes run up and down steep hills. On the steepest hillsides Pa usually planted corn because young cotton was so little that a plow would cover it up when dirt rolled on the hill. Fields lay bare in the winter. Pa improved his land by letting it lay out while weeds growed on it for a year. Then he added manure and plowed it under in the fall. When a field almost completely wore out, he turned it over to the pines. Then during the winter he chopped down trees and cleared a new ground. So much land was under cultivation that even in dry weather the rivers run red with soil and clay from the hills. Now most of the farmers is gone, and the rivers run clear in wet and dry weather all the year long. But somehow them that own the land now seem to love it less than the old farmers who was ignorant.

One time when we had a few acres of new ground to clear Pa invited the neighbors to a log rolling. They brought axes and saws and worked a day without pay. Ma and Lucy and the women served dinner, backbones, ribs, turnips, turnip greens, and punkin pies. The logs that could have been taken to sawmills just rotted and wasted. They was no sawmills close by and not enough logs to move a sawmill to the farm. Nobody ever hauled logs to a sawmill on a wagon.

One job Pa hated was plowing the garden. It didn't bring in money nor make feed for the stock nor meat and bread. He hoped Ma and a hoe would take care of the garden without him plowing it. But Ma never let him get by. So he'd have to guide old Kate through the garden gate, and Ma always reminded him not to let the mule stomp on the plants at the end of the rows: sage, rhubarb, pie plants, catnip, and castor-oil plants. The rows was short, Pa had to plow several different ways for the many kinds of plants, the fence didn't leave a place for Kate to turn around, she et the garden plants while Pa was thinking about the plowing, and Pa'd always get fed up and mad and say he didn't care whether the garden was plowed or not. From the time when Ma begun asking him to plow the garden until a few days after he had tried to do it, Pa was grouchy.

Plowing was a working agreement or a fight between a man and his mule or horse. Corn on good land had to be plowed till it was head high, and some plow animals could not be broke from taking a bite of the corn. Horses especially kept on eating even when they knowed they'd get a slashing. The temptation was more than the horse could stand. He'd try to sneak and slip a bite from a stalk of corn, but he'd get reckless and desperate and snatch a whole stalk out of the ground and break into a fast trot. Pa bought a fifteen-cent wire muzzle to cover the mouth of a horse that et corn, and some folks made muzzles out of poultry wire or strips of hickory bark. Some plow animals learned not to eat in the field. Once a mule was broke from eating corn, he never dared bite another stalk. He got sot in his ways; he'd give up the corn rather than have a whipping. But many a horse took a bite and begun running from the punishment even before he bit.

Insects worried horses and mules. Flies bit their ears until the inside of the ear was a solid sore. Pa made cloth covers for the ears. Some folks believed that strong-smelling walnut leaves kept the flies away, and they put little walnut branches on the bridles. Late in the afternoon gnats swarmed. A man with sweaty and dirty hands and arms just tolerated the gnats instead of befouling his face trying to keep them brushed away. A horsefly punctured the skin to suck blood before the horse knew it was about. The only way to keep a horsefly off a horse was to kill it. Bill Compton didn't have a horse or mule, but he cultivated only a garden and a roasenear patch. He pushed an old homemade plow by hand. One time he plowed hard in his garden and then come in and told his wife that the horseflies was eating him up while he was pulling the plow and that he just had to come inside to get shed of them.

After a field had laid out for a year and growed up in tall weeds, they was a danger of snakes. In spring snakes sometimes rolled out of new-plowed ground at the farmer's feet. One time I plowed up so many snakes that I walked on unplowed ground at the left of the plow. Most of the snakes was copperheads, what we called rattlesnake pilots. But a snake was a snake, and we killed them all—spread adders, coachwhips, and black snakes. One time we swapped work with one-armed Joe Watkins's family, and a black snake six feet long crawled into the briars at the end of the rows and left his tail showing. Joe caught the snake to show us how he could pop its head off like he'd crack a whip. Joe held the snake by the tail and whirled it around his body a few times and attempted to crack it, but with one arm he wasn't able to pop its head off. Us children couldn't decide whether we was more tickled or scared.

The hardest work ended at laying-by time, when we quit plowing the crops. Pa and Rufe did odd jobs on the farm, worked for a neighbor for wages, and picked peaches. The younger children went to school for a little while. Work started again when we had to start pulling fodder.

Pa watched the corn close. When he couldn't mash milk out of the kernels and when part of the shuck turned brown, it was time to pull fodder. Hot weather made fodder-pulling one of the hardest jobs of the year. You reached up, pulled down the top of the stalk of the corn, and then stripped off the blades all the way to the dead leaves at the bottom. Moving up and down all the time was wearisome. When you had a good handful of blades in each hand, you tied a hand, broke off the top of a cornstalk, and hung the little bundle on the stalk. Pa always planted watermelons in the corn. Sometimes we stopped, found a watermelon hid in the cool grass, busted it open with a fist, gouged the meat out with our fingers, and et the melon as the juice run down to our elbows. Then the rough fiber of the blades of corn stuck to our hands and arms where the juice had run, and it was hot and sticky. Stickers from the blades of corn scratched your neck and made life mighty uncomfortable.

Fodder pulled one morning was hauled to the barn late in the evening of the following day. That pulled after dinner was stored two days later. To gather fodder, you had to wait for the dew after the sun had gone down. Dew softened the brittle blades of the corn so the fodder could be tied by the blades into bundles. Us children enjoyed going to the fields late in the evening, gathering up the fodder, and riding home in the early darkness on fodder piled six to ten feet above the wagon bed. Riding high on a wagonload of fodder, I always felt like I was a famous man living a dangerous life. You can't describe the good smell of new fodder, but I liked to smell it like new cloth or fresh-turned earth or burning cedar. The wagon swayed over little roads and around the sides of hills, and us children rested on top of the new fodder and looked at the stars.

Early in the fall we pulled fodder from the sorghum and hauled the cane to the mill. A mule pulled a long lever around the cane mill. The surp-maker fed the butt ends of stalks of sorghum cane into the two revolving cylinders of the surp mill. Juice run down into a large wooden barrel through a towsack strainer. At the bottom of the barrel the juice flowed through a bung hole and down a V-shaped trough to the boiling pan. Anybody that come to the mill drunk his fill of the sweet fresh juice from the trough. Henry Underwood said a good fill-up of cane juice cleans out a fellow's bowels and gives him a good appetite.

Gathering corn was mainly a matter of pulling and hauling. Us children picked up potaters or peanuts as Pa plowed them up, and we made potater hills for storing sweet potaters in the winter. But the hardest work in the fall was picking the cotton. All the children six and over helped. Girls had nimble fingers, and they could pick more than the boys. Each picker carried a long sack and usually I drug it along the ground and crawled on my knees so I wouldn't have to stoop over and get a back ache.

Two little children picked from the same row so they could keep up with the rest of the family. We all liked to stay close together to enjoy the company. Sometimes during a long day children played or wrestled and fought a little while. One time Pa hired the Burges, a colored family, to help us pick cotton at thirty or forty cents a hundred pounds. They talked to the Lord in the field and sung mournful songs which gave everybody the creeps. At the end of the long day when everybody was tired and weary, Mammy Burge talked to the Lord and asked him to look after them all and guide them on through the way. Mammy sang an old song, and the rest of the family hummed along with her:

> I am weak, I am weary, I am worn.
> Blessed Lord, take my hand, lead me on.

After all the crops was gathered us children started to school and Pa begun to catch up on odd jobs around the house. In real bad weather we set around the fire and rested and looked forward to spring and planting a new crop.

THE FINDLEYS

*Ab and Lou Findley and their three children, Liz,
Fannie, and Milo, lived in a little house with a big
log room and a weatherboarded side-room. The house
had two windows, but neither window could be opened.
Ventilation came through cracks in the floor, the walls,
and the roof (there was no ceiling).*

*Ab's broad face was covered with tanned, dry,
wrinkled skin that resembled old leather soaked in
water and dried too fast. His long yellow mustache was
stained by juice from chewing tobacco. Lou kept her
jet-black hair rolled up in a ball at the back of her
neck. She had no teeth, but she said she could chew
chestnuts and the meat of the toughest squirrel that
ever climbed a hickory tree. Milo had what Lou
called the wiggles; some of the neighbors said it was
St. Vitus's dance. He often abruptly stopped walking,
turned quickly around, and walked a short distance
before he reversed his direction again. He always
said his name was "Milo Absolute Toad-frog Jumped
the Railroad Findley."*

*The Findleys kept their bony yellow horse in a log
stable and fed him in a trough made of a split hollow
log. They grew patches of corn, peas, potatoes, and
they raised one small bale of cotton. They picked field
peas on the halves and pulled fodder from their
neighbor's sorghum cane, topped it, and cut it for
the syrup mill. Ab was paid two gallons of syrup for
a ten-hour day, and Liz and Fan each earned a gallon.*

Sorghum was good "sweetening," and they never spent money for sugar. Ab and his dog, old Loud, provided possums and squirrels and rabbits. After a snow rabbits were easy to find, and Ab sold a few at the store for ten cents each or bartered them for green bulk coffee. Food was plentiful in the spring; creases grew in the creek bottom, and the "salet" of creases boiled with a piece of fat meat was good. Lou cut up wild spring lettuce with early spring onions and covered them in hot grease. Poke "salet" was plentiful. Sassafras roots boiled with a little syrup made a good drink. It kept their blood thin and free-running and prevented the fever.

The Findleys raised a hog on scraps and slop from the kitchen, spoiled sweet potatoes, and weeds which Milo pulled from the garden. They had no cow, but neighbors who had a surplus gave them buttermilk. Most families did not drink a cow's milk before the new calf was nine days old, but Ab said milk was good when the calf was three days old. Every time a cow came in, the Findleys had nearly a full week's free and abundant supply of sweetmilk.

Ab said Lou's praying took care of the family. After supper on a cold winter day the red fire in the rock fireplace warmed the family, the cats, and old Loud sleeping in the corner. Ab chewed home-grown tobacco, Lou dipped from a box of Bruton snuff, and the children roasted "taters" in the ashes. Just before they went to bed Lou prayed for the whole family.

5

Farm Animals

Willie and Jenny Murphy had four boys and seven girls and Tobe, the mule. Tobe was a big yellow mule with a coat of hair that was short and sleek except in the cold months when his hair grew long so that Tobe could keep warm. Until the oldest son, Byrd, was big enough to plow, Tobe was the only mule Willie kept; then he bought another that was the color of a mouse.

Old Tobe always did his part of the work. He pulled the plow in the corn and cotton fields on the hillsides of the Murphy farm. He pulled the long lever of the syrup mill round and round to extract the juice from the cane that John fed to the mill. He pulled wagonloads of cotton to the gin. He hauled the wood to keep the house warm in the winter and the stovewood to cook the victuals for Willie, his wife, and the eleven children. He pulled the buckboard fifteen miles to the county seat to pay the taxes in the fall, and at other times he made the long trip when Willie had to tend to business at the courthouse. When the boys were old enough to court the girls, Willie bought a new buggy from Sears, Roebuck, and old Tobe gave up his day of rest so that the boys could call on their girls on Sunday afternoons.

Byrd grew up and became a streetcar motorman in Atlanta and then a railroad engineer. John left home to become a streetcar conductor and then a merchant. Roscoe moved to Atlanta to work in a factory, and Ernest became a minister. The girls married off. But old Tobe stayed on with Willie and Jenny and Iney, the youngest girl. As Tobe and Willie grew old, they slowed down. They still made trips to the store to swap butter and eggs for groceries, and to the blacksmith shop for Tobe to get a new pair of iron shoes, and to the mill to get the corn ground into meal for bread for the family and for Tobe also. In Tobe's last days his teeth grew long and irregular, and he could not eat corn or chew all the blades of fodder. Somehow he stripped the stems from the fodder and ate the softest part of the blades. Twice a day Willie fed Tobe dampened corn meal. After Tobe died, Willie bought another old mule from a neighbor. He just did not have the heart, he said, to fool with the tricks of a young mule.

Like Willie Murphy, most farmers thought of their farm animals almost as human beings, and they loved them more than the land or anything else except their families. Many a farmer wished his dog or his horse or mule to have a temperament a little like his own, even when the likeness led to conflict. A stubborn farmer admired a stubborn mule, a grouch liked an old surly dog, and early-rising General Wheeler rushed a lazy rooster to the cooking pot. A mule or a horse had personality just the same as a plow hand. Some members of a family could handle a moody or excitable mule better than others could.

Usually the father plowed the work animal that was most difficult to control. Joe Watkins seemed to have a language that a horse or a mule could understand. With a few quiet words he could calm a nervous and frightened horse or mule. But no one could boss the Watkinses' mule, Old Pete, who always shied away from creek banks, little holes, and the end of a row. Pete refused to go near a hole dug by a dog looking for a rat or a

73

rabbit. He plowed a wide circle around it. Joe just had to give up the idea of plowing to the end of the row. But Old Charley, the Watkinses' horse, plowed wherever he was supposed to go—straight on into the ditch or the creek until he heard "Whoa!" He was obedient and had no fears.

A well-trained horse or mule easily learned where the plowman wished him to walk, and he could even lay off rows in a field where there was nothing to go by except the distance from another row. If rows were laid off in a curved contour, the horse or the mule learned to follow the curve of the previous row. Sometimes he needed the help of a gee or a haw. But it was hard to train a young horse or mule to walk in the correct place. Some old, untrained horses brought from the market in Atlanta just could not learn anything. Joe Watkins bought a twelve-year-old horse, Old Bob, and kept him for five years, but when he sold Bob he did not know any more than he had when he was born. Joe said, "Old Bob is just like some contrary men; you can't learn him anything. He's jist too dumb to learn gee from haw."

Some horses and mules were bad about stepping on the crops, especially in the short rows of fenced-in gardens. At the end of a row some swung around awkwardly and trampled a great space in the field. A big-footed horse killed many plants at the ends of the rows when he had to turn. Some plow animals, however, learned to take care of the stalks of cotton and corn, and they could even turn around in a small space between rows.

Some families preferred horses; some wanted mules. After a mule learned what he had to do, he never forgot, and he stubbornly carried out his own ideas. No matter what happened, he applied old rules until the farmer forced him to change. Horses had more sense than mules. Many a man hoped that his horse would reflect his standing in the settlement on Sunday when he drove a red-wheeled buggy or a two-seated surrey with a little fringe around the top.

Every farmer thought he was a good horse-trader, but somehow nearly all farmers lost money when they traded. Many a man was such a poor trader that his wife said he had "come to the bridle"; she meant that he had lost all he had in a hoss trade, and he had nothing to bring home or to start a new trade with except the bridle. Frank Patton, a tenant farmer, owned a little mule named Old Kate. A mad dog bit her, and Frank hurried to trade her off before she went mad. He swapped her for Old Jack, a little gray mule as wild as an antelope. But Old Kate did not go mad after all.

The Akinses' mule, Old Lou, was afraid of a stream. Once Roscoe tried to ride her across a branch. Two or three times when she came to the branch she lowered her head, bowed up her back, sidled around nervously, and backed away. With a look of you-just-don't-know-how-to-do-Old-Lou, Marion Akins told his son to get down. Then he climbed on her fat, slick back. Just before she was supposed to jump, he kicked her with his heels. Lou ran right up to the edge of the branch, stuck her head down to the ground, and twisted her tail. Then unexpectedly she jumped. Marion slipped off her back, landed in the branch, and dampened his enthusiasm.

One-armed Joe Watkins was drinking when he traded for old Charley, a chubby dapple-gray horse with a mis-shapen foot, and Joe did not know about the bad foot until the next morning. The foot was no handicap to anyone except the blacksmith, who had to learn to make an enormous horseshoe. Charley almost became a member of the family. He seemed especially to like Granny Watkins, who drove him to church by herself even after she was eighty. Every first Sunday of the month Charley clopped patiently up to a certain tree in the churchyard, waited patiently to be hitched, and waited again until

Granny came for him to carry her home. When anyone except Granny hitched him at the church, Charley broke loose and rambled about hunting for grass. Granny even believed that Charley knew that she could not see well. When her son told her that he was afraid for her to drive the two miles alone, she said, "The Lord and Charley will take care of me."

When Joe went to the county seat to pay his taxes, he always drove Charley. Joe's wife Palestine knew he would come home drunk, and she worried about him, but the children said, "Ah, Mama, old Charley'll bring him home even if he don't know his way." Once when little Hu Watkins was six years old he rode Charley to the branch. For two years after having scarlet fever, Hu had been unable to hear. He slipped from Charley's fat back, fell, and the side of his head hit a rock. One ear bled on the pillow most of the night, but the next morning Hu could hear with that ear. Years later a head specialist told Hu that such a thing could never have happened.

Charley was sensitive and temperamental. No one dared to carry a buggy whip when Charley was hitched to the buggy. Twitched with a whip, he jumped and broke the harness. Yet he instantly obeyed any soft command with the voice. If a back strap or a belly band of the harness broke or anything else caused what Charley thought was a crisis, he stopped and trembled until his master solved the problem. Plowing in the river bottom, Charley always could sense an approaching storm. Thunder and lightning caused him to nicker that he was ready to go to the barn. When the plowhand unhitched him and jumped on his back, Charley ran from the storm. As he grew old, his big feet stumbled easily, but somehow Charley kept the spirit of a colt while growing in the wisdom of the world.

When a farmer was trading for a horse or a mule, he always asked if the animals had ever run away. If so, he bought another or cut his offer twenty-five or fifty dollars. Mules ran away more often than horses. When a horse or a mule was badly scared, he lost all reason and ran. A runaway was as dangerous and wild as a jungle animal. Once Joe Watkins hauled a load of slabs without chaining them down. As the wagon went down a hill, one of the slabs slid off and fell against one of the mules. The desperate mule ran as fast as he could. Hu Watkins crawled backward on the shifting and sliding slabs and fell off the rear end of the load, but Joe was entangled in the slabs and the lines. Finally the mules reached home with only two wheels of the wagon, ran into the barn, and stopped. Joe's leg was broken so badly that the doctor never could set it exactly straight.

Jim Watkins's little black Texas pony, which had been branded on the Western prairies, was a fast runner. Turning around at the end of a row, the pony stepped one foot over the trace, lunged, and jerked the reins from Jim's hands. The pony ran four miles down the road with a single-foot plowstock flying in the air behind him. When the plowstock hung under the root of a tree in McFarland's peach orchard, he stopped. He was scarred badly, especially his legs. A sharp-pointed plowstock hitched to a runaway horse was a dangerous weapon.

Henry Harris kept the hairs on the tail of his old yellow mule Bob sheared nearly all the way to the tip of the tail. A mule with a hairless tail looked like an overgrown possum pulling a buggy. As Bob grew old, his belly grew bigger and his legs shrunk. He looked like a washpot with elongated legs. Henry drove old Bob when he went to pay his taxes at the county seat, twelve miles away. He never owned a buggy with a top, but he held an umbrella over his head to keep off the sun or the rain. Henry never trotted his mule. He said he saved money by taking care of his mules. Henry bought some small houses at Copperhill, Tennessee, seventy-five miles from his home in Cherokee County. Every month he saved his mules and walked barefooted to Copperhill to collect his rent. When he went to Marietta, thirty-five miles away, he walked to save his team. To keep from wearing out his shoes, he went barefooted.

A farmer who could not afford to buy a horse or a mule used a steer or an ox, the slowest creature that ever worked on a farm. Two oxen yoked together to pull a wagon were so lazy that they leaned on each other to avoid the effort of having to stand and walk alone. A team of horses or mules pulled a wagon three or four miles in an hour, but oxen loitered only one or two miles in the same time. Calvin Farmer owned two oxen, old Buck and old Darb. Old Buck was so lazy that he fell into the branch every chance he had. Calvin just had to let him stay down in the branch until Buck was willing to move.

Old man Marion (or "Marn") Wheeler owned one mule and a steer. He hauled lumber to be used for crates at the marble mill in Nelson, eight miles from Marn's farm. When he drove through Ball Ground, the people were amazed to see a mule trying to walk fast and an ox holding back. Once a family moved through the settlement with a wagon pulled by an ox and a milk cow hitched together. When they stopped to camp for the night, they milked the cow. Most of the folks who saw them had a feeling that somehow it was wrong to make a female cow work and to drink her milk too.

A farmer was tender with his beasts because he loved them and because he had to earn a living with their help. He watched carefully for signs of sores or sickness. Horses and mules often had shoulder sores caused by ill-fitting collars. During long months of idleness in the winter, shoulders grew tender, and sores were especially bad when work started again in the spring. The most common remedy was Dr. Porter's Healing Oil. It was so strong that a farmer could put it on a horse's shoulder in the morning and smell it all day long. The hotter the horse became in the heat of the day, the stronger Dr.

Porter's Healing Oil smelled. When medicine failed and nothing would heal the sore, the farmer bought a large collar and a thick cotton pad. To prevent the collar from pressing on the sore, he cut a hole in the pad where the sore was.

The cow and the garden belonged to the farmer's wife. Usually a family owned one cow for each horse or mule. A two-horse farmer owned two cows. So long as the cow gave two gallons of milk a day, the farmer did not care what kind of cow he had—whether it was half poodle or just a cow. Some had long horns, and some were "muley-headed." The wrinkles on the horn showed how old she was, a wrinkle for each year of her life. Most farms had a pasture with a shaky fence. The cow had to find her own living in the summer by eating whatever wild grasses happened to grow. Before the fence law, some had no fences, and the cow roamed over the countryside hunting for a place to graze. She wore a cowbell so that the family could tell where she was. The sound of the cowbell tinkling in some far meadow was one of the most lonesome sounds on the farm.

When a cow broke out of the pasture and wandered to a cornfield, there was hell to pay. Running a frolicky and stubborn cow was tiring, and the farmer despised the chase which took him away from more necessary work. The temperamental farmer beat the cow, thrashed the child who was supposed to watch her, and fussed with his wife. When old Pide broke into a neighbor's cornfield, sometimes there was a quarrel or even the threat of a lawsuit. But most quarrels were soon forgotten, and the next time the cow of one of the two "went dry," the other kept him in milk until the cow had a calf and "come in."

Some cows were especially "ornery" and wily in breaking through fences and frolicking over the country. General Wheeler owned an old raw-boned cow which, like General himself, refused to submit to any man. She would not even wean her calf. General put quinine on her teats, and the calf still sucked. He put a muzzle with sharp stickers on the calf, and the cow still let the calf suck though the blood ran from her udder. Stickers and the bitter quinine together failed. He put them in separate fences, and the cow jumped a four-foot fence to get to her calf. Finally General sold the cow and led her to her new owner four miles away. General stopped at the store, and when he came home he found that the old cow was there before him nursing her calf. There was nothing to do but kill her for beef. General said he had just about decided he did not want any damn cow on his place, but Uncle Bud Wheeler, General's brother, told him that the cow took after her owner and that it was his best chance to see how contrary and stubborn he was.

Cows had many ailments. If a milk cow ate wild onions, dog fennel, or some other kind of strong-flavored herb, the taste of the milk was abominable. Gus Lovingood doctored sick cows and horses in the settlement. A thin and puny cow that had a dull coat of hair, Gus said, had the hollow horn or the hollow tail. A hollow horn, he said, was very painful. He cut the horns off or treated them with a little gimlet, an auger-like instrument about six inches long. He screwed the gimlet into the base of the horn like a corkscrew and then poured a stinking medicine into the horn. A cow which had no bone in part of her tail had the hollow tail. Gus treated a hollow tail by splitting it with a knife and letting out the poison. Then he applied tar or turpentine and bound the place with a white cloth.

Little knots sticking up on the back of a cow were grubs. The farmer punctured the knots and mashed out a grub that was perhaps an inch long. When the hide of a cow grew tight to her body, the farmer thought she was hidebound and sick. Gus Lovingood put lye soap on the back of the cow, pulled the skin back and forth, and worked the soap into the hide. Heavy pressure made the hide pop loudly and broke it loose. Then Gus told the owner of the cow to sprinkle salt on her back regularly so that she would lick her back and keep the skin loose. For milk fever, he pumped air into the udder through the teats with a bicycle pump. When a cow found a calf, Dr. Lovingood advised the farmer to feed her six bundles of fodder to fill her deflated belly.

Alf Price castrated most of the hogs in the settlement. Frank Watkins watched him a few times and decided to try his skill at the art, but in his first try he succeeded in completing only fifty per cent of the operation. Joe Byers castrated cats without help from anyone. He put the cat's head in a tow sack, doubled the open end of the sack back under the cat's hind legs, held one knee across the cat's neck and the other knee across its hind legs, and operated.

A farmer liked his dog to be a good watchdog, a loud barker, a good fighter, and a good hunter. Otherwise, he did not care what kind of dog it was. Marthy Willingham once saw a country boy with his dog in Ball Ground and asked him what kind of dog he had. "Half hound," he said, "half feist, and the other half is just plain old dog." His little sister said she didn't know what kind of dog it was because the dog's mama had two husbands. If a dog was not a bulldog, a bird dog, a cur, or a hound, he was a feist. Feists made the best squirrel dogs. And many farmers kept feists simply because they happened to be their dogs. Once or twice a day, the farmer threw the dog a left-over biscuit or a piece of cornbread, but the dog had to catch a rabbit and hunt some of his own food. Many dogs learned to suck eggs on the sly.

Percy Owens's big brown shaggy dog, old Jack, was an expert snake killer. He learned that a crawling snake which is not coiled cannot strike effectively. When Jack attacked a coiled snake with its head raised, he knew just how far it could strike at any enemy. Jack walked around a snake slowly, watching for his chance and keeping his distance. When the snake struck, Jack dodged, grabbed it in the middle, and shook it so furiously and so fast that the snake was almost invisible. One hard shaking disabled the snake. Jack would rest, and wait, and shake the snake again until it was dead.

After Henry Lee's dog, old Josh, had grown old and become slow, a snake bit him on the jaw. His head swelled to the size of a water bucket, and Henry gave him gunpowder mixed in whisky. Old Josh recovered, but his head stayed big.

The howling and whining of a black dog after midnight was a warning that something terrible was going to happen in the settlement. Once Pete Jordan's big black dog lay out in the yard and howled all night, and the next day Pete's neighbor, Oscar Kellogg, shot and killed another Negro boy over a ten-cent bet in a card game.

Lucius Bice, who rented the old Wheeler bottom land above the river bridge, hired Brutus and Gorman Brown to help him plant his corn. When the Browns arrived in the field early one morning, their four dogs fought Lucius's one dog, chewed up its ears, and whipped it badly. Lucius threw rocks at the Browns' dogs and beat them up pretty bad. Brutus and Gorman said nothing during the day, but they worried about Lucius's beating up their dogs, and that night they told their mother and sisters about it. The next morning Brutus, Gorman, the mother, and the sisters waited on the roadside for Lucius to pass by on his way to the bottom land. Lucius was a good fighter, but the Browns were small and frail. Words flew fast and loud. Finally Grandma Brown yelled in a quavering voice, "You're jist a old boar hog."

"And you're just a old sow," Lucius replied.

That ended the argument.

The dog caused the most terrible fears that ever troubled the settlement. Nothing frightened a family so much as mad dogs. When a strange dog passed by, mothers rushed their children into the house and locked the doors. A man walking alone at night carried a stick to defend himself against mad dogs. When a dog went mad, the hillman said, his tongue swelled, and he acted strange and ran with his head held high in the air. He left home for a day or two, people said, came back, stayed awhile, and ran off again and hid. Many a lost dog traveling hot on the road was mistakenly shot because some farmer thought he was rabid.

Many dogs had running fits. Barking and yelping, they ran, lay down, ran, lay down again, and jerked all over. Farmers did not know what caused the fits, but many believed that they could prevent the fits and rabies by cutting out a little worm which grew under the dog's tongue. Probably they removed the salivary gland. Actually about eighty per cent of the running fits, veterinarians say, were caused by Agene, a nitrogen trichloride used to bleach flour and to improve baking. Running fits were caused when the dog ate biscuits.

At Cherry Grove School one day a group of men were working on the road. A man over sixteen years old was required by law to spend several days a year working on the county roads. Fate (Lafayette) Holcomb was plowing in a nearby field. The men stopped to rest, and Fate sat on the rung between his plow handles and rested. A strange dog came by, and Fate ran into the woods. The dog chased him, and Fate's two big dogs ran after the mad dog and caught it. Fate said he "clumb" a tree, and the dogs ran on by. Later one of the other men shook the tree, and it was so rotten that it fell over. Fate always thought Providence held onto the tree a little bit to help him. He killed his dogs to keep them from going mad.

Ad Godfrey saw a mad dog when he was hauling tanning bark to the railroad station. With his ax he fought it off from his horses. His dogs jumped on the mad dog, and it bit them both on the ears. Ad chopped the dogs' ears off with his ax, and they never went mad.

Some people believed they could prevent rabies by using a caustic acid to burn out the wound. A mad stone taken from the stomach or "punch" of a deer was supposed to prevent and cure rabies. Henry Robertson was bitten by a mad dog, but he did not believe in mad stones. Henry was afraid to wait three hours for the train to Atlanta; he hired a driver and the two fastest horses from the livery stable. By telephone and telegram he made arrangements for fresh horses at every stop down the line. The two horses set out for Atlanta in a long fast lope. The people in the settlement talked about Henry with sympathy and horror, and they feared that he might go mad in spite of the shots to prevent rabies. But he did not go mad.

Only one man in the settlement ever had rabies, and he did not know that he had been bitten by a mad dog until it was too late for treatment. Sipp Jordan's female dog was sick after she had puppies. When Sipp tried to doctor her, she bit him. Then she disappeared. After Sipp became sick, he had fits when he tried to drink water, and the members of his family had to hold him down on the bed. His death was an agony.

Chickens on the farm were mixed breeds, combinations of white and black leghorns, Rhode Island reds, buff Orpingtons, domineckers, and a few game chickens, rose combs and topknots and big combs. Some farmers did not feed their chickens at all. They expected them to scratch around in the woods and to make their own living. They roosted in trees or on the buggy or the wagon in the barn. If the boys in the family used the buggy for courting, they had to work hard to clean off the chickens' night deposits before they went for a drive. Often in cold weather chickens' combs froze and turned black, and the frozen part of the comb fell off. After a cold night an old hen was sometimes found frozen under her roost in a tree.

A rooster was as independent as a mule. He crowed as long and as loud as he pleased. If a boy threw an ear of corn at a crowing rooster, he dodged without stopping his crowing. A farmer could tell what rooster was crowing as far as he could hear him. Some sounded as if they had swallowed a bug and it had hung in the throat. There were bass crows and tenors and sopranos, serious crows and comical crows. General Wheeler was especially proud of the crowing of his roosters. During the summer he kept several until they were big enough to crow and then he killed all of them except the three or four that crowed the most and the loudest. General liked the early hours in the morning, and he wanted a rooster to tell him another day was approaching.

Wild animals preyed on the chickens: the mink, the possum, the fox, and the long-bodied weasel. Hunters found clumps of feathers where animals had dragged chickens to the woods and eaten them. Hawks ate many chickens. When a man killed a hawk his neighbor bought him a new knife or invited him to come over and have a chicken-pie dinner. Sometimes the farmer fed his chickens nux vomica, from which strychnine and brucine are derived. He believed that any animal which was born with its eyes closed would die if it ate fowls that had been fed nux vomica. When Palestine Watkins found two dead hawks in the swamp, she said that nux vomica killed them.

When a farmer's wife saw a hawk, she ran screaming to her husband, and he ran for his gun. Clarence Spriggs lived in a little log cabin which had a low doorway. Once when he had a rising on the top of his bald head, his wife Sally saw a hawk and yelled, "Hawk! Hawk! Hawk!" Clarence grabbed the gun from the rack above the fireplace and started running. He failed to duck his head low enough and the beam at the top of the low door clipped off his rising. He yelled to Sally that he wished the hawks would eat every damn chicken they had.

A duck was such a poor mother that she was never allowed to hatch her own eggs. She would follow a nearby branch so far away that she and her brood could not reach home any more. Chickens were set on duck eggs, and an old hen with duck babies always had trouble. Her little ducks swam in a branch, and the mother clucked up and down the branch to babies that for a reason strange to her stayed in the water. She became a nervous wreck.

The Watkinses owned peafowls. The peacock's tail had five-foot feathers with beautiful colors. The spread of the tail of a strutting peacock was at least eight feet in diameter. Horses and mules passing on the road were frightened by the strange peacocks, and sometimes the children had to run and scare a peacock away from the road so that people could pass with their team. The peacocks roosted in a very tall tree. Miss Vashti Wilkie, who lived at least two miles away from the Watkinses as the crow flies, could hear them screaming at night. They could fly better than any other domesticated fowl, and they ran loose over a wide range, but none of them ever wandered away.

Children caught wild birds for pets. Jim Watkins caught two baby crows in a nest in the spring, a male and a female. An angry old hen with chickens attacked the female crow and crippled it. So the children named the crows Crip and Piert. When they tapped old mischievous Piert on the side of his beak with a finger, he shook his head and seemed to laugh. Piert was a nuisance. He would steal a ball of thread or a thimble or a little piece of cloth and hide it where Palestine Watkins could never find it. When fall came, the crows followed the family to the cotton fields. Piert flew along with one of the cotton pickers, lit on a cotton stalk, picked cotton from a boll, and dropped it on the ground. During Christmas week the two crows disappeared; probably some hunter mistook them for wild crows and killed them.

Charley Bell robbed most of the bee hives in the Sharp Mountain settlement. He said that he was born under a sign which made him immune to stings. When Charley was old a bee buzzed into the bowl of his clay pipe, and ashes flew like dust in a whirlwind. Charley slapped at the bee, knocked his pipe to the ground, and only the cane stem was left in his mouth. Then the bee stung him on his face. After that, Charley lost confidence in his sign and began wearing a mask.

General Wheeler kept a pet chicken snake to catch rats in his crib. The snake sometimes caught a small chicken to supplement his diet of rats. And snakes ate eggs. Lou Finley left the door of her smokehouse open in the daytime so that her hen Old Peck could lay in her nest inside. One day Lou heard something thrashing about in the smokehouse. She ran out and saw that a chicken snake had swallowed one egg, crawled through the handle of an earthenware jug, and swallowed another. The handle was between the two eggs, and the snake could not get out.

Mountaineers from Gilmer and Fannin counties hauled pigs into the settlement in covered wagons drawn by oxen and mules. They sold a pig for two or three dollars. Farmers who could not afford a Poland China pig bought razorbacks or long rooters. They had long legs, a thin body, and a long slim nose or rooter. Neighbors laughed at a farmer for buying a hog that was "mixed with the possums." Or they said he fed his hog from a bottle and made its nose grow long and slender. When slop was poured into the trough made of half of a split hollow log, the mountain pig scrooched up in a far corner of the split-rail pen and showed the whites of his eyes. After a day or two, the pig was turned loose to roam at will around the barn and the house. But when he began rooting up flowers and herbs in the yard, he was again shut up in the pen. Most mountain pigs did not weigh as much as two hundred pounds after the farmer had fed them a year. Good pigs, Poland Chinas, Guineas, Berkshires, and Red Hampshires, might weigh four hundred pounds before they were a year old.

About the first of September the farmer began feeding the hog more corn to get him fat for slaughter. Before hog-killing time, some hogs were so fat that their eyes closed. Justice of the Peace Joe Lyon took great pride in raising the biggest hog in the settlement. He bought one pig a year, and his wife baked biscuits for the pig until he was old enough to eat corn. Joe preferred boars to sows, and he said that the runt* of the litter was likely to make the biggest hog.

A few weeks before killing time the farmer bought a one-hundred-pound sack of salt and cleaned the meat box to be ready for the proper sign of the moon and cold weather. He invited a neighbor to help him on hog-killing day. They set two big iron washpots side by side, and the boys filled the pots with water. After the fire was burning well around the pots, the farmer shot the hog with a rifle or hit him hard on the head with an ax or a maul.

When the hog fell, the farmer stabbed a long butcher knife into the throat and the heart to make the hog bleed. After the hog stopped kicking, it was dragged onto boards covered with fertilizer sacks, and boiling water from the iron pots was poured over it. If too little was poured, the hair would not scrape off; after too much, the skin was tender, and the hair would "git set" and would not yield to the scraping butcher knives. The only way to remove it then was to cut it off or singe it off with fire.

After the hair was removed, the farmer stuck a hickory gimlet stick about two feet long under the leaders in the hog's hind legs. A sweep raised the hog high enough so that his nose did not touch the ground. Then the boys rinsed and scraped the skin to make it white and clean, and the expert hog-gutter slit the hog open and dressed the meat with his razor-sharp butcher knife.

At Wiley Cochran's house William and Rufus always stood nearby, waiting for the bladder. Wiley pressed the fluid from the bladder, scraped off the fat, and left a neck an inch long. The boys stretched the bladder to make it elastic, inserted a cane quill in the neck, and blew on the cane until their eyes almost popped out of the sockets. The balloon made from the bladder was a good toy. Some children put peas in the bladder, and they rattled after it had dried.

All the insides of the hog—the intestines, kidneys, liver, lungs, and heart—were dropped into half of a wooden barrel which had been sawed in two. In the frosty early morning these parts steamed, and the smell of fresh hog was strong. The mother and the girls scraped and cut all the fat off the intestines so that it could be rendered into lard, and then they carted the chitterlings off to be washed at the nearby spring. The farmer lowered the hog from the sweep to a table, cut it into hams, shoulders, middlings, ribs, backbones, and all sorts of meat. The edges of pieces of meat were cut off and ground into sausage. Almost every part of the hog was eaten—the liver, the kidneys, the heart, the head, and even the brain and the ears and feet and tail. It was almost impossible to salt down and preserve some parts of the hog, and after hog-killing the family for several days had a great variety of meat from the one animal. After a farmer killed a hog, he sent a good "mess of meat" to every close neighbor.

The meat which could be salted down cooled overnight on a long table in the smokehouse. The next morning, the farmer spread an inch-thick layer of salt over the bottom of the meat box, placed a layer of meat on the salt, and then filled the meat box with alternate layers of salt and meat. Sausage was stuffed into flour sacks or corn shucks and hung up in the smokehouse. The more the sausage aged, the stronger it smelled. By mid-winter a child could tell which of his friends had brought sausage to school in his dinner bucket.

Animals provided labor, food, and other necessities. But the farmer seldom regarded them as mere necessities. They were God's creatures, just a little less contrary and likeable than man himself.

Bud Wheeler was a bachelor. For two or three months at a time he stayed sober and quiet, but his week-long drinking sprees were the wildest drunks in the hills. Drinking, he was a carefree soul, good company to his friends, and a mortal terror to those he disliked. Once Bud slipped and fell when he was drinking. Old man Webb Roberts said, "Uh-oh, Bud, did you hurt yourself?"

"I don't know, and I don't give a damn," Bud said, "but I believe I broke my bottle."

Bud and Smilin' Ed McConnell were drinking companions. When Smilin' Ed became a popular hillbilly singer and joker on WLW, Cincinnati, the hillman's favorite radio station in the 1930's, he told stories about Bud. Smilin' Ed wanted people to be big-hearted and help their neighbors, and Bud was a good example. Staggering home drunk on a cold rainy night, he passed a deep gully. Over the sound of the cold flooding water he heard a moan. Bud lurched to the edge of the gully, held up his lantern, and saw his friend Ab Mulkey.

Bud asked, "Whass trouble?"

"I got down here in this red mud, and I can't git out."

"What kin I do fer you?"

"Git me out of here."

Bud pulled and tugged, but the ditch banks were steep and slippery.

"I don't believe I can git you out," Bud said at last, "but move over and I'll git down there and lay with you to keep you company."

Once Bud was telling a long yarn on the whittlers' bench in front of Roberts Store. Just as he opened his mouth to show how a fellow hollered when he got hurt, a tumblebug flew in his mouth. Bud forgot the story and never did tell how it ended. He just chewed up the bug and said, "Now, God damn you, see if you can fly in anybody else's mouth."

Bud said that he had been afraid only once in his life. In the Hightower Church Cemetery some of the graves had wooden shelters. After a long hard drunk Bud staggered into the graveyard and fell asleep in one of the unpainted shelters. When he awoke on Sunday morning, the church bells were ringing. Bud said he believed it was Resurrection morning and he had died drunk.

When Bud was a witness in a case against a bootlegger at the county seat, a smooth lawyer asked what time of the year it was when Snake Holcomb cut up Gid Walton. Bud said, "It was brandy time."

The lawyer said, "Tell the jury what you mean."

Bud said, "They know. I don't have to tell em. Don't you know when they make brandy? It's when the peaches get ripe. I thought all smart lawyers knowed when brandy is made."

A hard-shell Baptist, Bud believed that what is to be will be. When he was drunk he argued religion and preached. One night he visited Cliff Wheeler and talked for an hour without ever telling Cliff that he held a grudge against him. Finally Bud left. He rode bareback on a little mule that did not weigh more than six hundred pounds, and Bud weighed over two hundred. His legs almost touched the ground on each side of his mule. He found a high hill close to Cliff's home and began to preach. "Here I set astraddle of my mule, preaching the gospel. If I'da had the practice, I'da been a damn good preacher." On and on he preached about how people ought to treat their neighbors. Then he hollered loud enough for Cliff to hear him, "Cliff Wheeler," he shouted, "I would just like to beat hell out of you right now."

Bud believed in ghosts. One dark night Hu Watkins and Cliff hid in a briar patch on the high hill where Bud did his preaching. Bud came and started his sermon. When he paused, Hu and Cliff clanked trace chains together. When they rattled the chains, Bud listened; when they stopped, he continued his preaching and cursing. After much preaching and rattling and more preaching, Bud remembered his old grudge against Cliff, who had let his cows get out of the pasture and into Bud's corn. Cliff had not offered to pay for the corn his cows had eaten. Bud preached, "Cliff Wheeler is the damnedest sorriest man I ever knowed since I was born, and I was born a long time ago. Cliff," he hollered, "you're not fit to live. You're not fit to piss." Cliff had to listen. Bud never did know what caused the rattling chains, and Cliff never told him.

Bud hauled produce to Atlanta. A half-dozen wagons banded together and hauled chickens, cabbage, and farm products to the market. The men liked to have Bud along, and most wagons carried a cargo of whisky. In the wagon yards in Buckhead, now a suburb of Atlanta, Bud's friends filled him with whisky and waited for a stranger and a bully for Bud to fight. Bud liked to fight, and always he used the same strategy. He "got the bear holt on a feller" and squeezed a man until he was in great pain. One group egged on the stranger, and another talked Bud into a fighting mood. The fight ended when Bud's bearhold squeezed the bully into submission.

6

Good Neighbors and Good Times

Old Zack Thompson, a tenant on Cindy Starnes's place, was feeble and not able to plant and work his crop one year. Zack's wife Minerva tried to plow the hilly and rocky farm. She was old and fat, and the plowstock bounced and made her shake all over. Sweat dropped from her red face. She gripped the handles of the old homemade plowstock until her hands were as calloused as a blacksmith's. It took all her strength to follow the little black mule, and even her gees and haws sounded like a whisper. After the neighbors heard about her plowing, they helped her half a day every two weeks and cultivated her crop for her. Working together, the settlement could till an extra farm without a great deal of trouble. Once when John Vaughn was sick, his friends plowed and planted his one-horse farm in a single day.

Farmers swapped work so that families could work together and enjoy the company. If Willis Howell's fodder was ready to pull before Ernest Cowart's, both families pulled fodder on the Howell farm. They had a better chance to pull all the fodder before it was too dry. When Ernest's fodder ripened, both families worked in his field. One year the Watkinses swapped cotton-picking with the Cochrans. Both families picked the Cochrans' cotton first, and Wiley Cochran worked so fast that no one could keep up with him. Joe Watkins wondered whether Wiley would work so hard when he picked someone else's cotton. He did. He was that honest. In the evening when the children were all hungry and tired of dragging the cotton sack through the field, Wiley's small son Rufus always sang a lonesome song. He especially loved his Grandpa Porter and Jim and Frank Watkins. Over and over Rufus sang, "Nim, and Nank, and Danpa Poka, Nim, and Nank, and Danpa Poka." After Rufus reached manhood and married, he was killed by an exploding gasoline can when he poured gasoline on a fire. For a long time the Watkins boys could not forget Rufus's lonesome and haunting song.

After a farmer gathered his corn, he invited his neighbors to come to a corn shucking. Every family tried to send at least one member. Farmers tried to raise corn with some red ears and some red grains. A red ear which a corn shucker found counted a hundred; a red grain, ten; a blue grain, five. The shucker who reached a thousand first was the winner. Sometimes the host put a jug or two of whisky somewhere in the corn and provided a feast, usually chicken pie, spare ribs, and backbone. The women spent nearly an entire day cooking tables full of food. Adults ate first, and children who had to wait for the second or third table wondered if the grown-ups would eat forever. There were corn shuckings, log rollings, house raisings, quilting parties, and all sorts of occasions for work and play.

All the charity in the settlement came from friends and neighbors. Deacon Holcomb's two cows were killed by a bolt of lightning as they stood under a big oak tree in his pasture. Neighbors collected quarters and dollars and bought Brother Holcomb two cows. He made a list of the givers and said that he would give anyone who had a misfortune four times as much as he had paid on the cows. No farmer ever carried insurance. When a family's home and furniture and barn burned, neighbors came bearing gifts, canned food and dishes and clothes and quilts and even furniture. They contributed logs and lumber, helped to rebuild the house and the barn, and brought wagonloads of fodder and corn to feed the stock.

Neighbors ministered to the sick, laid out the corpses, and took turns sitting up with them all night before the funeral. One group tended the sick or stayed up with a corpse until midnight, and another sat up from midnight until daybreak. On "setting-up" nights in the winter, a pot of coffee was kept hot on coals at the edge of the fireplace. The watchers ate teacakes and gingerbread and sweet potatoes roasted in the ashes. One night when a group of several young people sat up with a corpse, Ina Belle Stovall stuffed herself with potatoes and peanuts. She dozed off to sleep, entered dreamland, and broke wind. After that, for a good while potatoes and peanuts lost their popularity on "setting-up" nights.

Borrowing, the old people said, was "neighboring." It was a long trip to the store and often a family had no money and nothing to barter. When a man ran out of kerosene (lamp oil or coal oil, he called it), he walked a mile or two to borrow a quart. People borrowed meal and flour and coffee and matches and sometimes in the old days even a shovel of coals to start a fire. When a man's cow went dry, his neighbor furnished him milk and butter until his cow "freshened." When the neighbor's cow went dry, he was repaid in milk and butter. Fruits, apples and peaches, and vegetables, beans and turnip "salet" and cabbages and tomatoes, were borrowed and swapped and given. A man who charged a friend for minor articles or services would have felt unneighborly.

Young people invented many games and had many parties: pound suppers and box suppers, candy-pullings and candy-knockings, and Sunday-night singings. To a pound supper everyone carried a pound of food. For box suppers, each girl prepared a box of food with her name inside the box, and it was auctioned off to the highest bidder. The proceeds from box suppers usually bought equipment for the school. A boy ate with the girl whose box he bought, and no one was supposed to know who had prepared any box. The girls dropped hints, some true, some false, and a boy was often deceived so that he would buy a wallflower's box. Sometimes a boy knew which box his girl had brought, and his friends bid high because they knew he would raise any bid; and he spent as much money in the auction as he earned in a month.

At candy-pullings on Saturday nights a big pot of "sorghum surp" was cooked to make candy. A boy and a girl pulled the hot and sticky sorghum candy until it turned light in color, and then they wound it up and twisted it and laid it aside to get hard. They greased their hands with lard or butter to keep the candy from sticking on them. A boy considered it a great pleasure to pull the hot syrup and to touch his best girl friend's hot sticky hands. At candy-drawings two dishpans were filled with sticks of candy of two or three different colors. The pans were covered with a cloth, and a boy and a girl were blindfolded. Each reached into a pan held by the parents and drew a piece of candy. If the two sticks were the same color, they kept the candy. If they were different, the boy had to put his back in the pan, and the girl kept hers. The game was played until all the candy was drawn from the pan. A boy asked a different girl to draw with him each time. He pointed and said, "You go draw with me." A shy boy was awkward and embarrassed when he picked a partner.

At a candy-knocking a piece of candy was tied to a string hanging from the ceiling. One person was blindfolded and handed a stick of wood. If he swung at the candy and hit it, he was given a stick of candy. Clyde Ridings said that the game "just gummed candy all over the house. Looks like people woulda done better than that, don't it?" In another game one person was blind-folded and released among a roomful of people. When he caught someone, he tried to guess who it was. The game gave a boy a chance to touch the girls, and that was about the only chance he had. It took a long time to catch them all and win the game.

Sometimes boys rolled up a big ball of rags and threads from old socks and soaked it in kerosene. At a party after dark they set fire to the ball and threw it from one to another. A boy who could handle the ball fast never burned his hands. Sometimes a boy threw the ball under the feet of a girl and scared her. The girls wore fuzzy outing underwear, and they were afraid that it would catch afire. No one was ever burned much with the kerosene ball.

Birds roosted in the numerous brushpiles which a farmer made when he cleared a new ground. Children invited their friends, boys and girls, to a bird knocking. Everyone brought torches, bundles of splinters or "fat" wood or kerosene-soaked rags tied on the ends of sticks or packed in a tin can nailed onto the end of a stick. Three or four held burning torches around a brushpile, and one stomped on the brush to make the birds fly out. The knockers swung limbs and brushes back and forth and up and down. As the blinded birds flew out of the brush, the knockers struck some of them down and killed them. The next day the mother cooked a huge bird pie.

A boy eating an apple counted the seed and said a poem which foretold his fortunes in love:

> One I love, two I love,
> Three I love, I say,
> Four I love with all my heart,
> And five I cast away.
> Six she loves,
> Seven he loves,
> Eight they both love,

Nine he comes,
Ten he tarries,
Eleven he courts,
And twelve he marries.

The love vine, a small yellow plant which grew on weeds, was a parasite without a root system of its own. Someone pinched off a piece of the vine, slung it over his head three times, named it after his girl friend, and tossed it on the weeds. If it lived, she loved him; if it died, she belonged to somebody else.

Hill people told tales and sang old songs about death and love and war and fate and mystery. Strange tales seemed far too real to scoff at when they were told around the fire at night. Ghost tales told of eerie lights, clanking chains, strange voices, and white figures. Country people told tales of wonder about strange or tragic events years after they happened. The river burst into the tunnels of the old Franklin Gold Mine while the men were outside eating dinner, and not a life was lost. A bridge groaned and moaned whenever a wagon crossed it because the Logan boy died there when his team ran away with a wagon load of pyrites from the mine. The mules and the boy were drowned in the river. And little seven-year-old Matt Prince jumped into the river and drowned himself when his sister Ettie May brought a bucket of water to the field and would not let Matt have the first drink.

Many women cried when they heard the song about little Mary Phagan, who was murdered in Atlanta in 1913:

Little Mary Phagan, she went to town one day.
She went to the pencil factory, to get her little pay.
Leo Frank, he met her, with a cruel heart, you know,
And said, "Little Mary Phagan, you go back home no more."

Tender-hearted Rosie Pinyan stirred the feelings of the lovesick young men of the settlement by singing and

99

playing on the old-fashioned pump "orgin."

> They'll tell you they love you,
>   They'll tell you more lies
> Than the sand in the ocean
>   Or the stars in the skies.

> I'll build me a cabin
>   On the mountain so high
> That no one but the wild birds
>   Shall hear my sad cry.

Lon (Alonzo) Wheeler's favorite tune on his mouth "orgin" was "Darling Nellie Gray." Lon was a lonesome bachelor, and he always was sad when he played the song and his sister Callie sang it. Lon and Callie did not know that Nellie was a Negro slave. Another love lament was an old minstrel song:

> Oh, my pretty quadroon,
> The flower that faded too soon.
> My heart's like the strings on my banjo,
> All broke for my pretty quadroon.

There were happy "foot-patting" tunes like "Little Brown Jug," "Turkey in the Straw," "Turkey Buzzard," and "Sally Goodin." On Saturday nights young folks liked a dance and string music and old fiddle tunes like "Hop Right, Lady." Some of the songs, like "Old Hen, She Cackle," had more spirit than sense.

> Had a old hen,
> Had a wooden leg,
> Best old hen,
> That ever laid a egg.

> Run round the house,
> Run round the barn,
> All she run round,
> Done no harm.

The serious and the devout and many of the old folks frowned on such light-hearted songs. They liked hymns. Sitting in her rocking chair, Granny Watkins sang in a broken voice:

> Every day, every hour,
> Let me feel Thy cleansing power.

Palestine Watkins always sang "Shall We Gather at the River?" as she worked.

> Yes, we'll gather at the river,
> The beautiful, the beautiful river,
> That flows by the throne of God.

Some hymns described suffering and the hope of the Christian religion:

> I saw a wayworn traveler
> In tattered garments clad
> And struggling up the mountain.
> It seemed that he was sad.
>
> His back was laden heavy;
> His strength was almost gone,
> Yet he shouted as he journeyed,
> "Deliverance will come!"

Once a year on a Sunday in June the county singing convention was held in a church selected by the president of the convention. It was a day of courting for the young people and reunion for the old folks. People came in droves by buggy and wagon and on foot. A horse or mule was hitched to every tree on the grounds. Those who could not find an unused tree hitched their horses or mules to wagon wheels. The loud braying of the mules and the nickering of the horses mingled with the singing in the church. Colts that had been allowed to follow their mothers rambled around the churchyard when they were not suckling.

Every family brought a big box or a basket or even a trunk of food. When dinner time came the women folks spread big white or flowery tablecloths on the ground and covered them with food while the men fed their horses and mules. Dinner was always late and the stock and the children were hungry. The children cried for a piece of pie, the mules brayed, the horses nickered, and the girls screamed when the boys teased them with lizards and small snakes.

All the well-known singers in the county came: Jim Smithwick and his son Reno, Joe Tippens, Homer Land, Lewis Hendrix, Virgil Gaddis, Arthur Hagood, the Green boys, Check Holcomb, quartets and trios and duets and Scylla Williams. Regardless of how many were singing or how loud, Scylla's alto voice could be heard and distinguished above all the others. Joe Tippens, a stocky short man, was always called on to lead the first song. Before starting his selection, he said, "If somebody don't object right quick I'm a-going to pull off my coat." Then he started singing "Beulah Land": "Blessed, blessed land of Beulah." When he reached the chorus, the great volume of song rattled the window panes. Lewis Hendrix, a jolly man who ran the livery stable in Ball Ground, led the old song "December's as Pleasant as May." Jim Smithwick, who had taught two-week singing schools all over the country, led the singing of the notes from the old *Christian Harmony Song Book* instead of singing a song with words.

A plump young widow from Lathem Town, Viola Sexton, stood in the front row of the singers facing the crowd at all the singing conventions. Her singing opened wide the eyes of all the men and made the wives glance at their husbands to see how they reacted to the widow's singing. When she reached the chorus in the rhythmic song about the ocean waves, some of the men were wafted out onto the briny waters of the deep. She sang and rocked to the tune of "rocking, rocking, rocking, rocking on the ocean waves." Her rocking body rhythm cast a spell on the men, bachelors and married, young and old. Most of the young men sat tensely quiet. Occasionally old Fleet Fossett had to break the tension. He hit his leg with his open hand, stamped his foot, revealed his toothless gums in a wet grin, looked to the back of the church, and winked. Fleet's wife Minnie kept her back straight while she stared at her husband. When the widow rocked into the chorus, the men rocked with her. They watched the approaching waves and held onto the gunwales of the boat. The words "rocking, rocking, rocking, rocking" grew louder and louder. The motion of the waves seemed to increase with every chorus. "Rocking, rocking, rocking, rocking, o'er the ocean waves." When the widow reached the word waves, her whole body strained, quivered, and trembled. The front end of the boat shot upward, and the splashing waves of the salt water almost capsized the frail boat. But the men clung to the gunwales.

Toward the end of the day the audience solemnly sang "Nearer My God to Thee." A business session of the convention made arrangements for June the next year. The president made a talk, and then everyone sang the parting hymn, "God Be With You Till We Meet Again." The convention closed with the old folks' tears, handshakes, and good-byes.

Hill people were eager to read, but books were scarce. When someone did buy a book, it was handed about all over the settlement. One Christmas all the Watkins children who were old enough to have a little money ordered a book from Sears, Roebuck. Nancy bought Mary Jane Holmes's novel *Lena Rivers*, and many women cried when they read it. Most families subscribed to *The Comfort Magazine*, a newpaper-like sheet that sold for ten cents a year. Most people read it from cover to cover, including the advertisements for patent medicines like Mother's Relief and Cloverine and Rosebud salve. Many could hardly wait for the next month's exciting installment of the continued story or a new yarn about bald-headed Mr. Bowser. A few families subscribed to the semi-weekly Atlanta *Journal* or the tri-weekly Atlanta *Constitution*. The county paper, the Cherokee *Advance*, was the most popular paper in the settlement. *Farm and Home*, which cost twenty-five cents a year, contained some fiction. *Grier's Almanac* hung on a nail by the side of the fireplace. The family read every word in it and followed its weather forecasts and its signs of the moon. Some kinds of writing were considered moral poison or "pisin." Ten-cent Wild West books and detective stories were generally frowned upon as immoral and corrupting. Les Perkins read so many fantastic books that he planned a trip to Mars.

Love in the novels and magazines did not follow as many customs as love between courting couples in the hill settlements. A boy wooing a girl visited her in her home, usually on Sunday afternoon. Most of the time the young couple sat and talked with her family. If they went to church together, they walked in company with a road full of courting couples. They might sit together in church or in a buggy in the churchyard so long as they remained conspicuously in public.

Girls married young, usually about fourteen or fifteen, but most young men did not marry before twenty-one. Usually a young lady married her first boy friend. When she became engaged, she always lengthened her skirt, letting out the hem a little at a time so that an abrupt change would not be obvious when she married. People first knew that Jessie Purcell was engaged to Arthur Moody when the women noticed that she was wearing longer dresses.

Parents were extremely strict about the marriage of a daughter. Many attempted to select the young man themselves. Nellie Holbert liked Gus Moss, who was from a good and respectable family. But her father, Homer, objected to the courtship. Gus came to the Holbert fields to see Homer when he was plowing one day and asked him, "What you got agin me that you don't want me going with yore daughter?"

"I ain't got nothing agin you, ay God," Homer told him; "you're just not going with my daughter."

Most of the young hill women were virtuous, but there were a few bastards and a few shotgun weddings in the settlement. Most men just paid off. The standard price at the turn of the century was fifty dollars, but later the boy had to pay about a hundred. The families of the guilty couple met together and decided what was right and just. The boy or his father paid the money, and the families continued to be friends and to visit each other as they always had. The child took the mother's name, but everyone knew who the father was. A bastard was not an outcast, but the mother had a hard life. People said she had a "bad char-rackter." She was turned out of the church, and if she continued to attend church, some moved and refused to sit on a bench where she sat. Even her friends refused to walk with her in the road or on the street.

The games and pranks of the boys and the men were sometimes wild. On Saturday afternoons they played ball at the school. The Bice boys especially liked baseball because it started fusses and fights that ended in bloody noses, black eyes, and bruises. The next day it was peaceful again, and all the boys were ready for another game of ball. Those who did not play ball on Sunday afternoons went to swimming holes, played, wrestled, fought, and killed lizards.

Possum hunts caused pranks and devilment. At ten o'clock one night Charley Wilkie hid near a high stack of lumber at a sawmill. According to plan, Hu Watkins and Bud Wheeler and a crowd of possum hunters sat down by the lumber pile and waited for the dogs to tree a possum. After a time a low moan came from the stacks of lumber. Lee Wilson's eyes widened in terror, and Gay Wheeler asked, "What's that? What's that?"

After a dead silence, the moan came again, then a shrill scream. The possum hunters sprang to their feet. Wrapped in a sheet, Charley ran screaming from the lumber pile. The boys fled from the creature for about a quarter of a mile before they stopped and tried to regain their breath and their senses. Gay Wheeler raised his ax and threatened, "I'll cut hell out of it with this damned ax."

To prevent danger, Hu managed to get the ax. The boys decided that the sheeted figure was a wild man. Just a few nights before this hunt, someone had seen a wild man slipping through the wilderness a mile or so up the Etowah River at Hogan's Pond. The possum hunters were scared, and some of them climbed trees. Horace Wilkie laughed until the sheeted figure began to chase him. The closer Charley came to Horace, the harder Horace cussed. The sole of one of Freeman McPherson's shoes came loose from the toe all the way back to the heel. He could hardly run, and those who had climbed trees heard the diminishing sound of the loud flip-flop of the loose sole. Lee Wilson yelled at the boys who had climbed trees and told them that they would have no way of escape if the wild man climbed the trees after them. They came down. Finally, Hu said, "Boys, let's all gather around in a circle and talk this over. We got to know what this thing is. If you'll stick to the finish regardless of what happens, hold up your hand." Every hand was raised.

"Well," Hu said, "let's catch him." They began chasing the wild man, and he ran from the possum hunters. They ran until they were all exhausted; the others let Hu and Bud lead the chase. Finally Hu managed to get close enough to Charley to whisper, "Charley, let us catch you." Then Hu caught him and yelled, "Come on, boys, we've got him. Remember, we've got to take care of each other in this trouble." None of the possum hunters would jerk off the sheet while Hu and Bud held the wild man, but when Bud finally jerked it off, every boy swore he had known that it was a joke all along.

Some families made whisky and drank it and sold it, but other families vehemently opposed stills and drinking. It was against the code to report a still to the revenue agents. But there were snoopers, branch-walkers, who received ten dollars for each still they reported to the revenue officers. One snooper moved to Conn's Creek from Dawson County. Before the winter was over, he disappeared, and they found his head in Dawson. His friends said that he had gone back to the branch one time too many. Buck Mullinax once told Homer Cochran, "Up this here little branch I used to keep a still year in and year out. I didn't run it all the time, because they wasn't no sales for the whisky. Oncet a year a revenuer from Cyartersville come up here, and ever time he wrote me a letter that he was a-coming. We moved out everything, and he come up and checked and went back. Then we was safe for another year."

"Folks in the Cherry Grove settlement," Clyde Ridings said, "didn't drink a whole lot of whisky. Uncle Wilson Revis would go out to the store and come back fed up and a-preaching. Ma would make coffee fer him to sober him up. He was a good feller, and when he got to drinking he had to preach. They wasn't no harm in him. He had a false door in the front of his homemade breeches, sorta like the winder in a old pair of union underwear—one button held it up on each side in front.

"Not many of us boys drunk whisky. If a feller went to a gathering where they was women, they would be shore that nobody couldn't smell that liquor on their breath. They'd ask somebody to smell their breath to be shore. 'Try it agin,' they'd say; 'try it agin'—several times. If they had whisky on their breaths, the girls wouldn't pay no tention to em. Now the girls help em drink."

Local elections were always amusing and sometimes dead serious. Jeff Cochran lived in the Conn's Creek settlement, where Josh Moody had been justice of the peace as long as the old men could remember. Some of the men at Ingram's Store decided they would have a little excitement about the election of the justice of the peace. They asked Jeff to let them put his name on the ballot so that Josh would have some competition. In the election Moody received just two or three votes more than Cochran, and he was so angry that he refused to continue in office. Moody did not want opposition. The men who thought up the joke had to beg him a long time before he agreed to continue as justice of the peace.

Fist fights broke out at polling places on election days. Almost all voters considered their vote a sacred privilege, but candidates sometimes gave a friend several bottles of white lightning to help the campaign. Bill Compton knew how to get his friend elected mayor of Ball Ground. The race, Bill said, was as tight as the bark on a sycamore tree. Everybody knew how everybody else would vote, and Bill knew which voters would get too drunk to go to the town courthouse to vote and how to time the drinking. Nineteen voters who had intended to vote against Bill's friend never arrived at the polls, and Bill's friend was elected by six votes.

In a later election Colonel Guy McKinney, a staunch Republican, made arrangements to haul the Pit Johnson clan to the polls in a Model-T Ford. Pit was the head of a family of twelve voters, and Colonel believed that giving Pit a ride would insure twelve votes for his cause. The first carload of the Johnsons arrived at the courthouse under the Colonel's tender escort. As Pit entered the door he exclaimed, "I'm a Democrat, ay

God, and I'm voting Democrat, and I want everybody to know it."

The main gathering place for idle men in the Crossroads settlement was the whittlers' bench under the sheet iron shed in front of Seaton Runyan's Store. The bench was made from a pine plank about twelve feet long. The legs in the middle and at each end were uneven, and the bench tilted backward and forward as the sitters changed their positions. From one end to the other the edges of the bench had been carved by the whittlers' knives. The ground around the bench was covered with brown and sticky tobacco spit. Several feet away from the bench were cud-like wads of old "chaws of tobaccer" and a few cigar stubs which looked, Hubert Holbert said, "like they was left there by a constipated boy who had et some pinto beans."

Wash Gaddis arrived early at the bench every morning. He was an overgrown puffy fellow with uncombed blond hair which was as long on his neck and around his ears as it was on the top of his head. Wash had to breathe through his mouth, and his open mouth and thick lips gave him a stunned or frightened look. Wash quit school when he was in the fourth grade. Sometimes he cut kindling for the widow Holbrook, drew water from the well to fill barber Cagle's tank, and hoed a few gardens, but most of the time, he said, he "jist wore hisself out a-loafing."

As soon as Wash arrived at the store he bought a pink soda pop and a five-cent moon pie, a big round brown glob of gooey pastry with a little white icing on the top. Wash sat on the end of the bench with the drink in his right hand and the moon pie in his left. He had a set procedure for his after-breakfast snack. He took a bite of the moon pie, chewed a moment with a squishing sound, shook the bottle of soda pop just a little, held it up to the level of his face, eyed the remaining contents, and took a swallow—then another bite of moon pie, the same ritual, and another swallow of the pink liquid. When the last bite of pie was gone there was exactly one swallow left in the bottle.

One wet soggy morning old man Fleet Fossett walked to the store from home in a drizzling rain. He watched Wash bite the moon pie, shake the bottle, and drink. "Wash," he said, "how in the hell can you drink that slop a wet morning like this?"

With his mouth full, just after a bite and before a shake, Wash retorted, "You ain't got a lick of sense—the weather don't change the taste of it cause it is in a weather-proof bottle."

One early morning Mack Lee bought three cigars for a nickel and settled down to smoke one on the whittlers' bench. Mack was just learning to smoke cigars, but he puffed away and blew most of the smoke through his nose. Half way through Wash's moon pie, Mack's face turned white and his eyes looked strange. He said that he had "et a big bait of catfish" for breakfast and it was making him feel peculiar. All at once Mack jumped up, the catfish squirted out of his mouth, and some of it splattered on Wash's shoes. With his stunned look, Wash just sat still. Then all at once he vomited the moon pie and the pink soda pop, but he held on to the bottle and the big brown pie and never rose from the bench. With both hands full, he wiped the drippings from his mouth with his sleeve. Then he took a bite of the pie and shook the bottle. Most of that day the whittlers' bench had several vacant seats.

The men on the whittlers' bench talked about the news of the settlement, swapped knives, argued politics and religion, and told stories. Some men in the settlement spent most of their spare time on the bench. On days when Tobe Martin did not work at the brick yard, he told the same tales over and over about the exciting coon hunts he and Melvin Lawson had before the train ran over their old dog Romeo and killed him. Thad Southerland often brought a basket of a dozen eggs imbedded in cottonseed to swap for coffee or tobacco. Thad sold Seaton Runyan a one-legged rooster along with some other fryers but did not mention that one of them had only one leg. One morning Seaton made up a yarn about a show man coming by and giving him ten dollars for the freak rooster. As Seaton started to walk away, Thad followed him, said that he was the one that sold him the one-legged rooster, and asked for half of the ten dollars.

Men and boys hunted a great deal when they did not have to work. Shells were expensive—about forty cents for a box of twenty-five. Possum-hunting was a favorite because the slow possum could be caught and did not require the expense of a gun and shells. Boys bought chestnuts from mountaineers and ate them on possum hunts. In the daylight, they were too wormy to eat, but when a possum-hunter saw a friend eating wormy chestnuts, he liked them better himself. Partridges were so small that they were considered hardly worth the price of a shell. Men hunted them on horses and mules. When they found a covey, one man got down from his horse and set a homemade net, which was about a foot high and twelve feet long with ten-foot wings on each side. The men drove the birds with the horses. If the leading bird walked into the net, all the birds followed him, but if the leader jumped over the net, all the partridges jumped over it. The birds never flew very far from a horse or mule, and after one trial the men just turned the net around, went around to the other side, and tried again.

The farmer and his sons caught rabbits in boxes and turkeys and rabbits in snares. Rabbits gnawed holes in the palings around the garden and ate the cabbages and turnip "salet." The farmer knew how to set a trap with a string and a loop at the rabbit's hole in the garden fence. The next time the rabbit came to the garden, the looped string caught him and hanged him in the air. Old Uncle Frank Moss could track a rabbit in the snow better than any other man in the Sharp Mountain settlement. If the tracks criss-crossed, he knew the rabbit had been foraging for food. Around brier patches Uncle Frank could follow his particular rabbit right on through numerous tracks. When the distance between the tracks increased to five or six feet, the rabbit was on its way to another feeding ground or to his bed. The best tracker kept his eyes out in front fifteen or twenty feet and tried to see the rabbit's eyes before it jumped up from its bed in grass or leaves or broomstraw.

One of the greatest pleasures of the hill people was talk. Freeman Weaver enjoyed talking more than anybody. He was a school teacher, and he had a long, thin, pencil-like mustache that wiggled in every direction when he talked. He knew everything about every person who had ever lived in the northern half of the county. He visited his neighbors to talk about history and politics and the weather. When Freeman drove through the settlement and saw a neighbor plowing, he stopped, hitched his horse to a tree, walked across the plowed field, stopped his friend, and began to talk. Sometimes he hindered the neighbor's work from the middle of the afternoon until dark. No one knew how to stop his talking. If a neighbor visited him in his field, Freeman followed him a half mile to the road, talking. The neighbor walked off a little distance, tried to get away, and then had to stop to hear Freeman talk. Then he came up to the neighbor to talk. A little at a time, they left the field, and as the neighbor rode away on his horse he could hear Freeman still talking.

Once when Freeman went to the blacksmith shop and the corn mill, he hitched his gray mule to the wagon.

While he talked to the men, someone outside hollered, "Mr. Weaver, your mule is running away."

"Sure enough," he replied and talked right on.

"I think he made the corner and turned up on the next road up yon."

"Well," Freeman said, "I'll see about it. I believe I can take the nearest cut through here and head him off." But he finished his talk with the miller before he chased his mule.

The Jordan family enjoyed life as much as anyone in the settlement. Hubert Holbert liked to visit his aunt and his four uncles. "My Ma's folks," Hubert said, "they was Uncle Bud, Uncle Adolphus—they called him Doll— Uncle Tom, and Uncle John—four boys that never did marry. My Aunt Ida Bell took a notion to marry a time or two, but she give up ever time because she said she couldn't leave her brothers. Aunt Ida Bell did the cooking, and the boys worked for a living. All the Jordans loved company and big eating. Lots of times they had as many as twenty-nine folks there to eat. They had a big time. On Saturday nights they'd have great big parties—big cooking and much string music.

"Uncle Doll was a school teacher, you know. He was a great big feller, and he taught in a whole lot of country schools. Ever time the big boys at a school run the teacher off, the members of the school board would come and hire Uncle Doll to straighten the school out and put the boys in their places. By the time Uncle Doll got through giving a bully a whuppin, he didn't have no more trouble in that school.

"Some of my aunts loved to dip snuff, but they never did let Uncle Doll know they dipped it. He was a pretty dumb-like feller in sich as that, and he was dead set against snuff. The girls kept snuff setting on the fahrboard and told Uncle Doll they kept it there for company. One time the whole family was setting around the fahr, and

Aunt Ida Bell fergot and spit right big.

"Uncle Doll turned around to her and said, 'What you spitting so fur?'

" 'Well,' she said, 'it's just hot water keeps a-comin up in my mouth.'

"Uncle Doll enjoyed making a trip to Atlanter on the train ever few months. He allus enjoyed innocent little jokes, and a whole lotta times when he went to Atlanter he played like he was deef. Oncet he went into a shoe-shine place, clumb up in a cheer, and made signs to show the little nigger boy that he was deef and dumb and wanted his shoes shined. The nigger shined on his shoes a little. Then he looked over to his friend and said, 'Ain't he the biggest son of a bitch you ever seen?'

"After that Uncle Doll quit playing deef and dumb.

"My grandpappy never would let the Jordan boys play with the Mackey boys. They was rough as cobs, but their daddy was a fine feller. One of the boys was electro-cuted in the state penitentiary. Grandpappy didn't know how to keep his boys from playing with the Mackey boys without making them think they was better than somebody else. He finally told them that it's not the idy that one feller is bettern another one, but it's the idy that some folks is bettern some folkses' ways.

"Yes, sir. Them was good old times. I never knowed any family that was as happy as them four old bachelors and their old maid sister."

DOC JONES

Harelipped Doc Jones could not talk plain, but he enjoyed hearing his friends try to mock him. Edd Cagle, a bachelor, was Doc's best friend. Edd argued that he could imitate him exactly and that people who could not see him would not know the difference between him and Doc. Doc said he did not believe it, but Edd said he would prove it if Doc was willing. "You are out of a night a little. Some night before you git home, I'll go to your house and see if I can't fool your wife." Doc agreed, but insisted that he be around to see how quick his wife realized that Edd was not her husband.

When Edd and Doc arrived at Doc's home, Doc's wife had gone to bed. Edd walked into the bedroom, called Julie by name, and talked with her a little while. Then Edd said, in Doc's voice, "Move over. They ain't room enough fer me to git in the bed with you."

When Edd began to pull off his breeches, Doc hollered, "Uh-huh, no, no, you've gone fur enough."

Edd told a joke about Doc taking care of his baby. When Julie was in the kitchen cooking supper, Doc called to her, "Julie, git the dishrag and come here quick; the baby has shit all over the floor."

7

Sickness and Homemade Remedies

Hill people thought no more about the causes of tuberculosis and typhoid than they puzzled about why a rose petal is red or why a bean blossom is white. Sickness might be providential chastisement or punishment for sin, and God mysteriously caused the good and the righteous to suffer. Epidemics of typhoid were pestilences which the Lord visited on the people because of their wickedness. Some people believed that sickness just happened without cause or plan.

People knew little or nothing about germs or bacteria; they despised nastiness from instinct or taste rather than from any connection between filth and germs. Overripe fruits and melons and unclean water caused diseases because they were filthy, not because they were infested with germs. There were no screen doors, and flies were considered more annoying than nasty. In some families, the baby slept naked on a pallet on the floor, and every entrance to the child's body was black with flies. Graves in the cemetery were short. There were more graves for children than adults. Between 1894 and 1909 five children were buried in the Perkins family lot in the Sharp Mountain Cemetery. Not one of them lived less than six months or more than eleven. An epidemic of scarlet fever shortly after 1900 killed many children.

The doctor's best medicine was his bedside manner. He healed the sick mostly by making them believe they could get well. But hill folk tried to do without the services of the physician except in times of childbirth and grave sickness. Even the low fees of the doctor were a great extravagance. People turned to homemade remedies. When Charley Patton said he had the "rheumatiz," Bob Ellis asked why he did not go to see Doc Saye. "It costs too dang much," Charley said, "and I can't afford it. It ain't a case of being stingy. A body's got to go by the money he's got, and I ain't got no money and nothing to swap Doc Saye for his treatment. Besides, Peggy Ridings's herb remedy is going to help me a whole lot, and she don't charge but just a little bit fur it."

Herbs were the chief source for remedies and cures. The hillman knew by name hundreds of plants, flowers, weeds, and bushes, and many plants possessed marvelous properties which would cure all kinds of diseases. Providence had put diseases into the world, and Providence had provided herbs that would cure any ailment if a man could just discover which plant to use for which ailment. The herb doctor did not know how the herbs worked, but he knew what some old granny had taught him, and both he and his patient believed in an herb's miraculous powers.

Most families grew medicinal herbs in one corner of the garden. The midwife and folk doctor Peggy Ridings grew catnip, hoarhound, and calamus, and she made long trips into the woods to gather plants. Some of her medicines were so strong that they would eat up regular cork stoppers, and she kept them in bottles with rubber stoppers.

Hot teas of all kinds were good for a man's health, especially in the spring. Granny Watkins said that anybody who did not drink sassafras tea in the time of the rising of the sap was foolish. It thinned and purified the blood and kept off diseases. Peggy Ridings gave all her children an annual spring rubdown with sassafras tea, and when a child became pale and had no appetite, she gave him pills made of pine rosin. Granny Watkins made spring bitters, a tonic, by boiling herbs in water: elder and wild cherry and alder bark, heart leaves, yellow root, the May apple, and pokeberry roots. Then she mixed the concoction with whisky and kept it in an earthenware jug with a corncob for a stopper. Spring tonics were made from the black roots and the yellow roots of the two kinds of sarsaparilla ("sassyparilly").

Herb teas cured diseases. A foul-tasting tea made from the roots of the boneset plant could "drink up" pneumonia. Peggy Ridings prescribed a small dose of kerosene for pneumonia, and she saved old Uncle Barber Henson's life with kerosene. Catnip tea cured colic in babies. Peggy sprinkled sulphur in it. Ginger tea with lemon juice or, better still, with a little whisky, was a cure for colds. A man drank the tea, went to bed, and sweated the cold out of his body. Tea made from life everlasting, or rabbit tobacco, cured a cold and relieved constipation. Pine buds boiled and then sweetened with honey or sugar made a good cough syrup. Red-oak bark taken from the north side of a tree, boiled in water, and sweetened with honey stopped coughing. Some mothers mixed water of tar with wild cherry bark and honey. Children who had a bowel trouble were given a tea made from peachtree bark scraped off the limb with an upward motion. Scraped off the limb with a downward motion, the peachtree bark made a tea to stop vomiting. Three "messes of poke salet" eaten in the spring prevented typhoid fever all the summer. Dr. Hawkins offered to treat typhoid fever free of charge if the patient had eaten three messes of poke salet the previous spring.

A powerful medicine was needed to make the measles break out and to lower the temperature. Margaret Howell used buttermilk and salt and black pepper. Angie Holbert made cornfodder tea. The best remedy for the measles was sheep manure tea, but some families argued that rabbit pills were as good as sheep pills. Most mothers gave their children two tablespoons of tea four times a day without telling them what the ingredients were. Measles struck Jess Tatum's family. Jess's wife believed in the old remedies. She boiled sheep manure pills and made her three girls and three boys drink the tea. Jess fussed with his wife for mistreating the children. Finally, Jess himself caught the measles. He was determined to go on with his farming because the measles, he thought, could not be very bad. Jess laughed at the sheep manure tea, but his measles did not break out. He became so sick that he was afraid he would die. At last he asked the children to go to Preacher Bell's for sheep pills. It was several miles, Jess was sick, and he could hardly wait for the children to return. When they did get back, he said, "Ma, you go ahead and make the tea, but I'm so sick I can't wait. Give me some of them-air pills so's I can be a-chawing on em while you're biling the tea."

Peggy Ridings made worm medicine out of Jerusalem oak weed mixed with syrup candy and made into pills. Some mothers boiled the seeds of Jerusalem oak weed and made a liquid worm medicine. Vermifuge, a dark brown bitter syrupy medicine bought at Roberts Store, was used to get rid of worms.

Granny Watkins cured dropsy with a span of bitter herbs (that is, what she could hold between her finger and thumb), a span of spruce bark, one of yellow sarsaparilla, one of red alder bark, one of dyeleaves, and a lump of saltpeter the size of a bantam hen egg. She boiled the ingredients, put them in a gallon of whisky, and then added a little rock candy. Three drams a day cured the dropsy. Judge Jim Brown, who was badly afflicted with dropsy, went to a number of clinics in Atlanta. Grandma tried to get him to take the old remedy, but he refused. He told the Atlanta doctors to send him home when they saw that they could do no more and that he was going to die. When they finally did send him home, he tried the old remedy, the swelling disappeared, and he had no dropsy at all when he died. Laura White said Granny's remedy cured her.

To cure the hives, Mun Smith used a little gourd about the size of a charger that powder was measured in for a muzzle-loading gun. He split a little place in the child's skin over the backbone, used the gourd as a suction cup, collected the blood, and gave it to the child to drink.

Fainting was a common ailment of the hill women, and perhaps sometimes it was feigned to attract attention and sympathy. A woman who fainted lay on the floor unconscious and pale and looking barely alive. Every family kept a "faint bottle" with whisky and camphor in it. It smelled strong enough to awake the dead.

Salves and poultices and liniments were good medicines. A tar poultice was a good treatment for pneumonia. Peggy Ridings and Granny Watkins both made their own tar. They chopped up rich pine splinters, dug a hole in a clay bank, set the pine afire, placed it on a flat rock so that the tar would run out onto the rock and into a container, and then placed a pot over the pine so that the tar would boil out instead of burning up. They weakened the tar with lard so that it would not be strong enough to blister the skin, covered a cloth with the tar and lard, and used it as a poultice on the chest.

Granny Watkins told a story about a man in South Carolina who was dying with pneumonia. It was eighteen miles to the nearest doctor, and he had to come on horseback. When he came, the only way he could tell that the sick man was alive was by placing a glass over his mouth. Moisture collected and proved that he was living. The doctor told the family that he doubted that the man would live until the next day. "If I don't hear from you tomorrow," the doctor said, "I'll take it for granted that he is dead, and I'll not be back." The next day they sent for the doctor, and when he arrived he said that something had happened to the man and that it was not caused by anything which he had done. Then they told the doctor about a tar plaster that some old woman had put on the man's chest, and it had cured him.

Granny Watkins's old remedy for the piles was made from wall ink, a plant that grew in the edge of water. She boiled the wall ink in water until it became what she called an ooze. Mixed with lard, it was used as a salve. Juice from a heart plant also cured the piles. Judge Jim Brown, brother of Governor Joseph E. Brown, had such a bad case of piles that he had to sit on a feather pillow, but Granny Watkins cured him in a short time. France Wheeler's daughter Nelly had the piles, and Joe Watkins prepared the herbs for her without charge. She hurt Joe's feelings when she told a neighbor that the medicine was not any good. He said that as far as he was concerned her tail could rot off before he would give her any more medicine.

At one time or another nearly every child in school had the itch. Some families kept the itch year after year and seemed never to be much bothered by it. Calvin Farmer said his children could catch it quicker than anybody, but the Roberts boys never had the itch. Once Calvin told Carl Roberts, "You ought to have the eatch jist one time. You jist don't know how much pleasure it is to scratch." When Calvin's daughter Zona Lee (she was named for her mother, Arizona) caught the itch, he took her to Doc Saye and said, "We've got the eatch; have you got some medicine that'll cyore it?" Dr. Saye gave her a salve, but Calvin told Carl Roberts that he knew a better medicine: "If you ever catch the eatch," he said, "go to a poke stalk and dig out the root, slice it up, and boil it good. Bathe in that poke juice, and if you don't shit in your breeches I'll give you a quarter. The streaks of eatch will swell up, and if your ma don't hold you you'll run jist like fahr was on you and jist like turpentine was poured in your bottom and hit rubbed with a cob." Hubert Holbert tried the poke juice remedy and said, "Big old whelps come up on me big as match stems, but hit didn't cyore the eatch." When Palestine Watkins's boys caught the itch, she boiled homemade tobacco, mixed the nectar with lard, and greased the children with it. Many people gathered the buds from balm ("bam," they said) of Gilead bushes and made a salve. Some used black gunpowder and lard to cure the itch; others tried sulphur in lard as a salve or sulphur and the white of an egg.

Country boys let their hair grow long, and lice were hard to find and kill. A month after school started, Carl Roberts's mother held him down over his school slate and combed his hair. If he had any lice, she could see them crawling on the slate. Some mothers covered the head in kerosene to kill the lice; others washed the children's heads with corn whisky. Old Bill Compton said he could not imagine a sweeter way for a louse to die. Louse grease was a blue patent medicine which came in a little tin box. Clyde Ridings said it gummed up the hair like tar for a month. Some just mashed the lice between their fingers. Once Ras Hamilton sat behind Gooney Mull in church. Gooney was completely bald-headed except for a little fringe around the edges. He kept scratching his head in the little patches of hair, and finally Ras said to him, "Run it out in the open and I'll swat it for you."

The rough life on the farm caused many risings, felons, and sores. Dew poison was especially bad. If a sawbrier scratched the feet early in the morning and dew wet the wound, the farmer had a bad sore. Dog days and fodder-pulling caused sores. Polly Farmer treated sores with a salve made of sheep tallow and turpentine. Angie Holbert boiled marigolds in water, mixed the ooze with lard and sulphur, and treated sores with the salve. To cure felons, people scraped the bark of seven bark and mixed it with meal or flour to make a poultice. A piece of fat meat or spider webs mixed with red mud were good for risings. Some broke an egg and used the membrane (which they called "scrivin" or "scriffen") just inside the shell as a medicine for risings. These remedies "drawed the rising to a head." A mason dirt dobber's nest wet with vinegar made a good treatment for risings and a poultice for sore throat. The mason dirt dobber built a big long nest and filled it with spiders and bugs. The dirt in the nest seemed to be especially powerful.

Walnut hulls cured ringworms. Athlete's foot, which the country people called toe "eatch" or toe itch, was treated with a poultice of cow manure, preferably hot from the cow. Octagon soap and turpentine removed corns and callouses from the feet. Someone told the Woody girls fresh cow manure would remove freckles. They tried it the week before protracted meeting to look especially pretty, but it dyed their skin green.

A man who plowed in the hot weather, sweated a lot, and used a cob for toilet tissue would get chafed, or "galded," he said. As a cure, he used elder leaves instead of cobs. Sometimes a man's crotch became so "galded" that he could hardly walk, and some used flour as a powder to help cure the "galding."

To stop bleeding, people scraped a felt hat and put some of the fuzz on the cut. Smut or soot (the farmer said "sut") mixed with sugar would stop the flow of blood.

An old Bess bug, a big black creature found around an old rotten log, contained one drop of blood in its body. Dropped into the ear, that one dab of blood brought quick relief for the ear ache. George Houston had a bad ear. He said that God put flies here for a purpose. So when he lay down to take a nap he turned his infected ear up so that the flies could eat the corruption that came from his ear. George said they purified the sore.

Two ex-slaves, Pete Jordan and Capus Gober, treated venereal diseases. A hunter often saw where Pete had dug up the roots of a red haw bush or gathered the berries. Pete would never tell anyone his medical secrets. At night colored men and white men from places as distant as Knoxville, Tennessee, came to his little one-room cabin for treatment.

Rufus Blackwell said bleeding would stop when the guilty knife was stuck into the ground. Once Bulldog Roper cut Gooney Mull, who was just a boy, in a fight, and Gooney was about to bleed to death. When Bulldog reached home and told his mother, she asked for the knife and ran out and stuck it in the ground. The blood stopped flowing a few moments afterward. If a boy's side hurt while he was walking, he stooped over, picked up a rock, spit on the bottom of it, and laid the rock back just exactly where it was. When he raised up, his side had quit hurting. Some men conjured off warts. They spit under rocks or rubbed the warts with a dishrag and put the dishrag under the doorstep or tried some other spell. Henry W. Ingram was the best wart-remover in the county. He once conjured twenty-seven warts off the bag of Kendall Champion's cow.

Many believed that a strong smell killed the germs of typhoid and measles and some other diseases. When two or three in a family were sick, the mother often cut up a plateful of onions and set them in the dark room with the sick. Or she skinned the peeling from an onion, tied a string to it, and hung it up in the room. The onion helped the sick to get well, and the members of the family who did not have the disease could enter the room and avoid the germs because of the powers of the odor of the onion.

Durm Hardwick said he was a good doctor. Once a week he made the rounds of the settlement and asked at every house if anyone was ailing. Lottie Jordan saw him coming once and told her children, "Don't tell him I stuck a nail in my foot." When Durm asked, "Is anybody ailing?" one of the children said, "Ma stuck a nail in her foot." To prevent lockjaw, he told her to smoke her foot over a fire of burning woolen rags. Lottie said she had no wool, but Durm went home, brought some dirty wool rags, set them afire in a bucket, and made Lottie sit on the edge of the porch and hold her foot over the smoking and stinking wool rags.

During epidemics children wore asafoetida to prevent measles, mumps, and other diseases. A piece about the size of the end of a finger was tied in a white rag and carried on a string around the neck. It had a foul odor, though often a child could not smell it above the body odors in the schoolroom.

Rabbit tobacco, or life everlasting, was a cure for tuberculosis. After it dried it had a soft, white, long, narrow leaf which was velvety in texture. Tuberculars made a pillow of life everlasting and slept on it to cure their "consumption." A copper wire prevented rheumatism. Old Rip Hill, who was afflicted with rheumatism, always wore a bright copper wire around his wrist to keep from having attacks of the "rheumatiz." Buckeyes carried in the pocket also prevented rheumatism and served as a good luck charm. A man who placed his shoes under the bed at night with the left shoe inside the right one would not have the cramp in his legs. Nellie Holbert made her children sit under a chicken roost to dry up the chicken pox. Her brother Hubert asked her if she made them wait until the chickens dropped something on them and said he thought that ought to cure any disease, but his question made Nellie angry, and she asked him, "Don't you think I ain't got no sense?"

Joe Watkins's father was killed in the Civil War two or three months before Joe was born. People believed that a man who had never seen his father could blow his breath into the mouth of a child and cure the rickets or the hives or the thrash. Strange women who lived far from the Sharp Mountain settlement brought their babies to see Joe, and he went out to the wagon or the buggy, reached over, and blew his breath into the child's mouth. Joe did not believe his treatment did any good, and he did not charge a fee. When he blew into a baby's mouth, he blushed and looked guilty, and his eyes seemed to ask, "Poor woman, why do you believe such a thing as that?"

A madstone was supposed to prevent rabies, to draw out the infection when it was placed on the bite of a mad dog. The greenish madstones came from a deer's "punch," the stomach. If it stuck to the place where the man had been bitten, that proved the dog was rabid, and the stone prevented the man from going mad. Faith Cochran advertised his madstone every week in the county paper. People came from as far away as Alabama to be treated. It looked like a worn creek rock about the size of a partridge egg with a chip broken off one end. Faith dipped the stone in milk and stuck it to the wound. After it had sucked out the poison, it dropped off the wound.

The best cure for snake bite was a live chicken. Old man "Marn" Wheeler was bitten by a copperhead or pilot rattlesnake while he was grabbling sweet potatoes. He grabbed a chicken and disembowelled it and put it on the place where he was bitten to draw out the poison. The trick was to split the chicken open as quick as possible without bothering to wring its neck or cut its head off first. When Doll Owen was bitten by a snake, she saved her life in the same fashion, and she said that the chicken's body sucked out so much of the poison that it turned "green as pison."

A hillman did not know that he could buy contraceptives, and if he had known about them, he would have been too embarrassed to ask a merchant for them.

Many women believed that a woman could not get pregnant as long as she was letting a baby nurse. Some babies were not weaned until they were five or six years old. Bill Compton told a yarn about Mark Chumbly nursing his mother until he started to school. She tried to wean him by putting asafoetida on her nipples. Once in church Mark cried for his "dinny," and she let him nurse while he was standing on the floor beside her. He took a few draws and started to spitting. He said, "Pa, give me a chaw of backer. Ma's been eating wild onions and I've got a bad taste in my mouth."

When a mother could not nurse her baby, a woman who had a baby about the same age took care of both babies. The milk from a mother who had a baby several months old caused a new baby to have the colic. If no alternate mother was available, the family boiled cow's milk and fed it to the baby in a spoon.

Midwives delivered the babies, and sometimes a man waited on his own wife during labor. Gus Lovingood, a horse doctor, delivered four of his children without any help from doctor or midwife. Peggy Ridings charged only $2.50 for delivering a baby until about 1890. Then she raised her fee to five dollars. She delivered all the babies in the Cherry Grove settlement until she died at age eighty-two in 1899. There was no doctor closer than Gainesville, forty miles away by horseback. It took a doctor so long to get to the Cherry Grove community from Gainesville that a seriously sick patient might be dead before he ever came. The people had to have midwives or someone who could provide immediate treatment for the sick. Finally, Dr. Robertson settled in the community. The Martin brothers practiced under him, went with him on his calls, and learned to be doctors. When Dr. T. J. Martin started practicing on his own, he was called to see a sick little baby in Centersville. It cried constantly, and no one could do anything for it. Dr. Martin looked at the baby and found a cockleburr in its clothes.

He slipped the prickly seed out and gave the baby a dose of some useless medicine. The community then believed that he was an excellent doctor.

For years and years Dr. Hawkins was the leading doctor in Ball Ground. Calvin Farmer still enjoys talking about Doc Hawkins: "One time," Calvin says, "he started to Uncle George Nicholson's, where he was a going, but he had been out on the road so much that he went to sleep. The horse come right on up to our house and stopped. Ma waked Doc up and said, 'Doctor, what's the matter?' He said he wasn't sick; he had just started to Uncle George's and went to sleep. I think the charge for delivering me in 1877," Calvin says, "was two or three dollars. Once ever one of my folks but me had the fever, and Doc Hawkins come down there seventy-five or a hunderd times, and he just charged us a dollar. My brother Jerry hauled pole wood out of the woods down there up to Doc's house. He hauled about a hunderd loads to him to pay the doctor bill. He had a pile of wood as big as a good-sized house. Old Doc would take yearlings, hams, wood, chicken, meat, eggs, or anything on his bills."

Dr. J. P. Saye was a friendly physician who was loved by all his patients, but he was also reserved and impersonal in many ways. A short stubby man with an odd beard, he kept his chin cleanly shaved and left long whiskers on each side of his face. Regardless of the hot weather, he always wore a black coat, a shirt which was always clean and stiff with starch, and a narrow black bow tie.

Doc Saye was an orphan boy. He lived with his Grandpa and Grandma Spears near Sharp Mountain Creek on a small, rough, hillside farm. He attended a one-room log schoolhouse, then struggled to attend the town school. He had no money. After he finished school, he had to borrow five hundred dollars to attend the

Georgia Medical College, from which he obtained a diploma after one or two years of study.

Before 1888 Doc Saye established his office in a room in his home in Ball Ground and tacked up a sign in bold letters: DR. J. P. SAYE. No one in the town knew what the initials stood for. Jack Purcell had the nerve to ask the good doctor what his full name was, and old Doc's face had utterly no expression as he replied in a clipped voice, "It's none of your business." Years after the doctor died his oldest son told someone that he believed the initials stood for Josiah Paynie. In the doctor's office, plank shelves lined the walls from the floor to as high as he could reach. On the shelves stood unlabeled amber gallon jugs and bottles of pills of all colors and sizes. The odor of the drugs seemed to mingle the smell of decayed flesh, iodoform, a hint of perfume, and mysterious odors. No patient ever knew what kind of drugs Doc gave him except when the prescription was for calomel. The only reason Doc told a patient he was taking calomel was that it was necessary for him to take a purgative four hours after the calomel to keep from becoming salivated.

Doc Saye kept four horses, two black ones and two white ones with red eyes. He drove them to the buggy in pairs, the blacks together and the whites together. One of the blacks was a trotter, and the other was a loper. When Doc was making a hurried call, people could recognize the unmatched rhythm for a mile. His buggy was always covered with red mud from the roads. Day or night, he never refused to make a call, even during his old age when young doctors refused to leave their warm beds. The settlement had no telephones, and people seemed to wait until dark to get sick. Lawson Town, across the river from Gober, seemed to have more sickness than any other settlement. After dark, someone on a mule galloped for the doctor, and forty-five minutes later a family who lived at Gober could hear the mismatched team. The doctor's horses were fast, and ten minutes later the man on his mule came following the doctor to the bedside of the sick.

When Dr. Saye arrived at a home, he hitched his horses to a tree in the yard, walked peppily to the front door, and said as he reached for the latch string, "Shall I come right in?" From that moment the patient seemed to absorb the doctor's good cheer and energy and to feel better. He strode to the bedside of the patient, asked a few questions, looked at the sick person's tongue, put a thermometer in his mouth, leaned over and listened to the chest, and counted the pulse as he watched his big gold watch. The watch had a lid which opened when Doc pressed the winding stem down. He carried it in his vest pocket attached to a heavy linked gold chain with a dangling gold fob. The doctor's examination of the patient was an anxious moment of suspense for the members of the family, who sat or stood in a doorway watching.

Finally the doctor made his diagnosis. Then he opened his big black square satchel, which carried his full line of drugs, asked the mother for an empty bottle, filled it with a strong-smelling drug, made up capsules from white and yellow powders, and gave directions. Then he asked the farmer about his cattle and crops, told a good joke, laughed heartily at his own humor and good spirits, and said, "I'll be back day after tomorrow." Behind him he left new hope for the sick and the family. When Doc left, they felt that all would be well.

Doc Saye's first wife, Angie, often went with him on calls out into the country over the rough, hilly roads. Angie said that when Doc had hitched the horses to his buggy to make a call on a patient seriously ill he dropped onto his knees before entering the buggy and asked God to help him treat the patient. His prayers were short; long-drawn-out talk was never a part of his life. Once during a revival in the church the preacher called on Doc to lead in prayer. Slowly and solemnly, he knelt down in front of his bench, paused a moment, and prayed, "God, have mercy on everybody. Amen."

Once when Doc was delivering a baby in Andy Cockriel's home in Lawson Town, Andy said, "You keep your hands off my wife. She's mine, and you ner nairy other man ain't gonna tech her." Doc snapped his black bag, rose, and said, "You deliver the baby yourself then," and walked out the door. Andy had to change his mind fast and beg hard before Doc would return and deliver the baby. All babies were born at home, and Doc charged a five-dollar fee. Frequently the mother would have bed sores before she was allowed to walk two weeks after the baby was born.

Doc had an old secret Indian remedy for appendicitis. He never operated, and he had the reputation of never having lost a patient because of appendicitis. People came from cities far and near to get Doc's treatment. Charley Hendrix took the Indian remedy when he was about to die, and he recovered. Later Charley said that for several hours after he took the medicine he could feel something pumping hard in his belly.

Doc Saye could stop typhoid if he could begin his treatment in the early stages. He broke the fever up with two calomel tablets followed in four hours by a big dose of castor oil, a treatment which made a man so sick that he believed he was going to die. When the climax came, Tom Evans said, "Lots of stuff poured from both ends. That old puke stunk like cyarn. My bowels jist run off like a squirt gun." The sick man turned white, sweated, trembled, and "talked out of his head" for a while. Old Aunt Julie Chumbly said that if typhoid was caused by a germ it was impossible for a germ of any kind to be alive inside of a fellow after a round of calomel and castor oil.

Walking fever was a slight case of typhoid that left

the patient able to walk around. Eating overripe water-melons or bruised fruit that had started decaying would cause typhoid. Only a few persons believed that flies or a contaminated well could cause it. Aunt Ida Bailey said trusting in the Lord would keep it off.

Once Doc Saye treated Mrs. Robinson for several days, but she did not improve. He became uneasy because her "summer bowel complaint" was getting worse. After he had given her every medicine that was supposed to cure the disease, his wife suggested that he try blackberry wine. In desperation he left a large bottle of the wine labeled "Take ten tablespoonfuls every three hours." Next morning, Mrs. Robinson exclaimed as the Doc entered, "Doctor, I'm a gitting jist about well. That new medicine you gave me tastes exactly like blackberry wine."

"Yes, ma'am," he replied.

For stubborn cases of rheumatism, Doc bled the patient, punctured a blood vessel on the inside of the arm just above the elbow, and let the blood stream out into a pan. Bleeding, he said, drained off the polluted blood so that new and pure blood would take its place.

Doc's first wife spent several months in the state hospital for the insane. Doc's home burned, and he hired a carpenter to build another home just exactly like the first one so that she would not be disturbed when she came home.

Almost all the time old Doc was in a good humor, but sometimes during an epidemic, strain and overwork made him grouchy. One night Tom Prince woke the Doc when he had not had enough sleep for several days. Tom spoke carelessly, "Doctor, my tooth is just a-killing me and you've got to pull it."

"I don't have to do any such of a damn thing," Doc said, "and if you don't get out of here I'll kick your ass."

After the automobile came, Doc gave up his horses and started driving Model-T Fords. When the Model-T gave way to the Model-A, Doc was getting old, and he did not wish to learn to drive cars with new-fangled gear shifts. He wrote a letter to Henry Ford and asked that the Ford Motor Company sell him four new Model-T's to last him until the end of his days. But Model-T's were out of stock, and Doc had to learn to drive the new cars. He did fairly well except when he started the car. For some reason he thought that he had to give it a good warm-up in the morning. When he cranked the car, he held onto the steering wheel rigidly, left the car out of gear, and stomped the accelerator all the way to the floorboard. The deafening roar of the motor could be heard for two miles.

Until Doc Saye was eighty he ran the one hundred yards from his barn to his house once a day with the wind and speed of a young man. Doc's son Maynard struggling along the street by his fast-walking father looked like a much older man. Doc's age remained his secret until the end, and no dates were placed on his tombstone or those of his two wives who died before him. Jack Purcell once told Doc he was eighty years old and asked if he wasn't just a little bit older than the doctor was. Doc replied, "You can be just as damned old as you want to be, but my age is my own damn business."

In the 1930's all the physicians in the county organized a county medical association and arrived at several agreements about their practice, including standard fees for office calls and house calls. All but Doc Saye. He joined, but he told one of his fellow physicians, "Bedamned if anybody or anything is going to tell me how to treat my patients and what to charge them."

One night Boogermole Boling broke into Doc Saye's chicken house, and the Doc heard his hens cackling and shot his shotgun in the general direction of the disturbance. Early the next morning Boogermole knocked on the doctor's door and said, "Doc, I've got some shot in my back. Would you pick em out?" Doc Saye picked out his own shot, never sent the vagrant Boogermole a bill, and never was paid.

The last generation of people Dr. Saye served seemed to believe that he was as old as the world. He was the balm of Gilead, and when he died, the community without him seemed to be a void. For Dr. Saye, the group of settlements he served was world enough. He was loved by his neighbors even though he never allowed anyone to know him personally.

"Eyeglass peddlers" brought satchels full of all kinds of spectacles into the hill country. Anyone who believed that he needed glasses just kept trying on different kinds until he found the pair he could see through best. Once a peddler went to Nebraska Bagwell's house, but none of his glasses helped her to see any better. Nebraska, a young woman, wanted glasses to add dignity to her appearance. The peddler had one pair of frames without lenses, and at last he asked her to slip them on. "These," she said, "are the best ones I've tried on yet." She bought them. The tiny oblong lenses in the old-fashioned glasses were so small that the eye could see through them only by looking horizontal and straight ahead. The best pairs had bright gold frames, but the cheap ones were made of brass which corroded, turned green, and stained the skin of the face.

When a man's tooth became rotten enough to hurt, he went to a dentist and had it pulled. Sometimes a farmer owned tooth pullers and extracted teeth without any pain-killer of any kind. The general practitioner also pulled teeth. When Doc Saye pulled a tooth for Joe Watkins, another tooth clung to the one he was pulling, and the good doctor pulled two at the same time without any additional charge.

When Callie Mae Wheeler had a severe, throbbing toothache, she went to see old Doc Gunter, a nervous and shaky dentist who was addicted to drink. Doc never filled a tooth; he just pulled—and charged fifty cents for each extraction. When he administered a local anaesthetic, he held the needle with both hands so that he could keep it steady, like old Tomp Heard shooting a crow. The end of Tomp's gunbarrel wiggled in a nervous arc a foot in diameter. He timed the wiggles and knew when to pull the trigger, and he killed a crow nearly every time he shot. Old Doc Gunter tried to watch for the right time to poke the needle in, but he missed and hit the back of Callie Mae's tongue, jerked out the needle, then rammed it into the bone below the gums, and broke it off. Callie Mae jumped out of the chair and said, "To hell with you and your damned toothpulling. I'm going to a dentist who's not a old drunk son of a bitch."

BLUE BOLING

Blue Boling was a short fat fellow with a big nose, a good-natured neighbor, and the best joke-teller in the settlement. He had jokes to tell to the preacher and the deacons and jokes to tell when the church deacons were absent. Jokes for children, and even some for the ladies. He saved some special jokes for the grave-diggings in Sharp Mountain Cemetery. When Blue visited sick neighbors, he came bearing jokes. The more serious the sickness, the milder the joke.

Blue was famous for his jokes even when he was a boy. One of his little friends once pulled up his shirt and showed Blue his navel (he called it his "nabul") and said, "Look where a Indian shot me."

"Your whole family," Blue replied, "has had Indian trouble. That's not half as bad a scar as your mama has got just below that."

But Blue never told a joke or said a word when he was drunk. His wife and children escaped during his violent drinking and spent the night in the local school-house, in the woods, or in a neighbor's home. For a while at the first of a drunk Blue locked himself up. Then he took his gun and killed the chickens. Or he beat the dogs and the cats. No one ever understood how Blue could be so good-natured when he was sober and so mean when he was drunk.

In his last days Blue became very religious. A few weeks before he died he was baptized in the Etowah River when he was too feeble to stand up.

8

Signs and Mysteries

When the farmer returned from the barn after feeding his stock before breakfast, he told his wife about the signs he had seen. "They's a red sunrise this morning," he would say. "We'll have rain before three days." When there was no red sunrise, he commented, "Looks like we're gonna have a few more days to catch up with our plowing and hoeing cause there ain't no sign of rain this morning." After a long rainy spell, he said, "I heard a bird singing back over on the Holcomb Hill across the creek. I guess the rain is about ended and the weather will clear up soon." The whippoorwill and the raincrow were important sign-givers; their calls were heeded carefully. The raincrow was a weather forecaster, a predicter of rain. When the whippoorwill cried his lonesome night call in the spring, warm weather had arrived to stay.

If the sun set behind red clouds on Wednesday night, there would be rain before Sunday night. A red sunset on a night other than Wednesday had no such meaning. When the sun rose behind red clouds on any day of the week, rain came within three days. When the moon in one of its quarters had points turned downward so that the moon-vessel would not hold water, the earth was to have rain; and if the points turned upward so that water would not spill out, there would be a dry spell.

Roosters were supernatural. General Wheeler often spoke of the crowing of the cock in the Bible. After a rooster crowed in an unusual way or at an unusual time of the night, something bad happened. If a neighbor was seriously sick, General would say, "I wonder how old Tom Wilson is; you know that rooster crowed peculiar last night." Crowing hens predicted calamity. People killed them because they were unclean agents of evil. A few who would not eat a crowing hen sent a son to the store to barter a dozen eggs and the unclean hen. They let someone else eat her.

The farmer studied the moon, watched it carefully, read about its phases in his almanac, and believed that it controlled many aspects of life on earth. He planted his crops according to the signs of the moon. If corn was planted at the wrong time of the moon, it grew a big stalk and a little ear. Planted at the right time, it produced a good yield on little stalks. Beans planted on the wrong time of the moon would "go to vines."

Ab Finley said he could look at a cornfield along the road and tell what stage of the moon it was planted in. Ab and Jim Watkins drove to the county seat in a buggy, and every time they passed a field of corn, Jim asked, "What kind of moon was it when that was planted?" Ab became confused and troubled about some fields, but finally he collected his wits and said, "That field was planted about half way between the right time and the wrong time."

During the summer when the sap was up, most farmers cut wood "on the full of the moon." Timber cut at that time, they said, drove the sap out of the wood. It cured out white and was not stained by the sap. Wood that was pretty and bright burned well. Cordwood cut on the old of the moon would never cure just right. Because of the sap and the wrong sign of the moon, it was damp and "sobby." Pulpwood cut in April and May and on the right sign of the moon could be peeled easily with a hoe that had been straightened. Later on in September all the woodsman had to do to peel wood cut on the right sign of the moon was to use his ax and make the bark fly off. The bark on pulpwood cut at the wrong time of the moon stuck tighter than the skin on a hide-bound bull.

It was especially important to kill hogs by the signs of the moon. Hogs killed at the new of the moon had more lard in them than hogs killed on the old of the moon. Homer Holbert believed that he could kill a hog at an exact time of the moon so that the meat would be all lard or at another exact time to make it all lean meat. Homer decided what kind of meat he wanted and then killed his hogs accordingly. Wiley Cochran believed that the time of the moon did not determine the kind of meat, but he argued that in hogs killed on the new of the moon the fat and the lean separated well, and it was easy for his wife to render out the grease.

There was a time of the moon to castrate hogs, to catch fish, to go hunting, and even to dig a hole. Dug at the time of a full moon, a hole had less dirt in it than a hole dug any other time. If a man died at the quarter of a moon, gravediggers had a hard time. They had to throw great quantities of dirt out of the hole, and after the corpse was placed in the grave there was so much dirt that it could not be shovelled back into the hole. The gravediggers had to haul a huge pile of dirt out of the cemetery.

A few men argued that there was no basis for the beliefs in the signs of the moon. The Ridings family discussed the subject for hours with their neighbors. Clyde Ridings still tells stories about how his family defied the moon: "My grandpa and my pa did not believe in signs of the moon. We cut wood on all times of the moon, and we allus burnt ever bit of it without any sign of bad wood. Other folks claimed that wood cut on a

139

wrong time of the moon would turn blue and sobby and wouldn't burn well. When we planted our corn we planted it in the ground when we got the ground ready and did not wait for any sign of the moon. Early corn allus grows short, and late corn allus grows tall. The year will grow higher up on the stalk on late corn, and that's what causes folks to git all mixed up about the moon. My daddy castrated hogs all the time without ever knowing what the sign of the moon was, and he never did lose one. He always wanted a frosty clear morning to keep the flies away. Other people said that a boar castrated on the wrong sign of the moon would bleed too much. They wanted the sign of the zodiac in the almanac to be somewhere besides in the privates when they castrated a boar."

Once Lola Worley told Lucy Ridings: "My ma is the one that learnt me how to make good sauerkraut. She told me and I've watched it every since. She said if you make it on the right time of the moon it will always be good, but if you make it on the wrong time of the moon it will stink."

"Well," Lucy said, "you know how old Lum Bell stinks; I guess he was made on the wrong time of the moon."

The hillman's beliefs about the moon seemed mild compared to the moral convictions of some of the strictest folk, the despair and certainty of a severe Baptist, and the predictions of doom and Armageddon by some of the religious prophets. Margaret Howell whipped her girls if they even asked her to let them go to a dance. Once when company came Charley Howell sang "Barbara Allen." After Sweet William died for the love of Barbara,

> She looked to the east,
> She looked to the west,
> She saw the corpse a-coming.

Charley sang:

> She looked to the east,
> She looked to the west,
> She split her corset a-coming.

Before she could sing another line, her mother sent for a peachtree limb and "whupped" her while the visitors listened to her yelling.

Rance Wilson was a hard-shell Baptist. He believed that what is to be will be and that God elected a few for salvation and predestined the many to hell. God, Rance said, had damned him to hell without a chance. By nature Rance was a sad man, but he had a good time. He said he was going to raise enough hell to deserve to go there. And he did.

During a blackberry winter, a cold spell late in the spring, Uncle France Wheeler, a hard-shell Baptist, was driving home from carrying a load of lumber to town. As he passed Les Baldwin's place, Nancy Baldwin was working in the garden, covering her early beans with old sacks and papers to prevent frost from killing them. Uncle France reprimanded her, "If hit's the Lord's will for your beans to get killed they will, and if hit ain't, they won't." Nancy quit covering her beans after she had protected two rows of the four. The next morning she had two rows of dead beans and two rows unharmed by the frost and the Lord. Mack Holcomb argued it was wrong to flee to a storm cellar, because "the Lord," Mack said, "holds the wind in his hand." Henry Lee argued with Mack: "The same Lord that holds the wind in his hand also made rattlesnakes, and hit's a man's duty to use the brains the Lord give him to shun dangers."

A few homemade prophets in the settlement read the Book of Revelation, foretold the time of the battle of Armageddon, and identified the NRA and its symbol of an eagle as antichrist or the beast. Whatever happened, it had been described specifically in the Bible and es-

141

pecially in Revelation. Miss Roxie Green's hen laid a prophetic egg, which bore the writing "End of time, May 15." Miss Roxie told her neighbors, and the children were terrified and fearful for weeks. When Halley's comet came in 1910 many people prophesied that the end of time would come when the tail of the comet set the world on fire. On the day when the comet came closest to the earth, many prayed and hid in their storm cellars or fled to the church.

A ghost was almost as real as a person or a sweet potato to many old timers. Clanking chains, rolling balls of light, and voices of the dead predicted calamities. Granny Watkins told stories of haints that prowled around on lonesome nights. One stormy night while she and the older children sat up weaving cloth, they heard a warp on the rooftop. After a strange stillness, they heard a warp again, louder than before. Then came the third and last warp and a terrifying commotion on the board roof. Granny said she told her children that the warps were a warning that some tragedy was coming—three days later death came and carried away Joe Lumpkin's baby boy.

Cliff Scott said he saw a ball of fire descend from the heavens three nights in a row. It settled gently into the trees beyond Cliff's barn, rolled smoothly across the roof of the barn, floated up and down across the yard, and vanished into his brother Wesley's room. On the day after the ball appeared the third time, Cliff found his brother dead in the woods beyond the barn. He had drunk strychnine, and while he was dying he had wrestled down a pine tree four inches in diameter and walked around and around with the tree until he nearly wrung it off the stump. Cliff always said that if he had just known what the ball meant he could have saved his brother from suicide by sending him to the insane asylum.

Aunt Em Wilson was a jolly old widow who lived in a little one-room shack which stood in the woods a half mile from the road in the Cannon settlement. During the winter she looked enormous because she wore a tent-like dress with numerous layers of petticoats underneath. She visited a great deal because she did not wish to be alone. Wherever she went, she wore an old-fashioned apron with an enormous bib. It was so large that it covered almost all her dress except above the waist in the back. When Aunt Em was a bride, her husband hanged himself from the limb of a blackjack oak. Anyone in the community could point out the tree and tell the story about how it had never grown an inch since John hanged himself. The children were terrified when they heard the story about John Wilson tying the rope around his neck, tying it to the blackjack oak, and jumping off a limb. No one ever knew why he committed suicide.

After John's death, Aunt Em began making long visits with her neighbors. When bedtime came, she placed herself in front of the fireplace in a rocking chair and asked the family to put on a big log of firewood to give her heat through the night. One night when Aunt Em was visiting the Watkinses, they had a house full of company, and Hu had to sleep on a cot in the room with Aunt Em and the fire. Several times during the night he woke up. All night long Aunt Em prayed, worked her lips, murmured her prayers, and said magic verses. She said that she had difficulty breathing and feared that if she lay down she would smother to death in her sleep.

George Ann Patton and her husband Frank lived in a log house at the foot of the hollow about a quarter of a mile below Sharp Mountain Cemetery. Their water came from a spring not far from the graveyard. George Ann said she knew that the water did not drain from the graves because it was not greasy. Up in Lumpkin County where she was raised there was a spring with water that ran from graves. It was greasy just as if it had a little lard in it. George Ann went to most of the buryings at Sharp Mountain, and she could always tell whether the next corpse brought to the graveyard would be a male or a female. After the new grave was filled up, she watched to see the first person leave. If a man or a boy left first, the next one buried would be a male, and if a woman or a girl left first, the next would be a female.

Martha Jane Wigginton's daughter Sally married Rafe Cochran in the early morning so that they could catch the nine o'clock train and go on their honeymoon to Chattanooga. Martha Jane warned her and Rafe because it had always been known that a "wedding before ten would come to a bad end." Sally stood Rafe's drinking and "cuttin-up" for three years before she quit him. A year later she married Amos Ledbetter in the early morning. Again her mother warned, "A wedding before ten has a bad end." But Sally consoled her mother: "After living with Rafe three years, I think that 'before ten' stuff is a good idea. I may need to git shed of Amos quicker than I did Rafe."

For years the county convicts camped close to Sharp Mountain Church when they worked the roads in the northern half of the county. Shortly after 1900 a guard whipped a convict to death because he refused to work, and some people said that the poor criminal had been sick with typhoid fever. He was buried in Sharp Mountain Cemetery. Because he was a convict, they buried him north and south instead of east and west like the other graves in the cemetery. The mound on his grave sank far into the hole within a few days after the burial, and during the next few years the gravediggers had to fill it several times. Now it has disappeared; curious old-timers search for it, but can find no sign that it ever existed.

A few families and older people refused to believe in spirits and ghosts. Calvin Farmer tells a story about a tenant who was afraid of "haints." "My pa bought the Byers place. It was a good house, but the tenant, old man Key, he wouldn't live in the house. He lived in a sorry, leaky old house up on the hill. After night, he said, you could go to the Byers house and hear the chains in the house a-rattling. We moved into the house that was supposed to be hainted, but nothing ever bothered us. In them days a man had to get grown and able to do his own thinking before he would refuse to believe in ghost stories."

The Leonard family believed in ghosts. When they moved into the Gaddis house, Josh Covington collected ten terrapins and put them upstairs in the loft. The Leonards started to move because ghosts were always scratching and crawling around in the attic, but Josh told them they ought to look in the attic in the daytime. They found the terrapins, but they never did understand how terrapins had climbed to the top of the house. Everybody thought the Nix house was "hainted" because they heard a pecking, pecking, pecking in it all the time, but then they found out that an old polecat was making the noise every night.

Deathbed stories told in the hills were more fearful than the ghost tales. If a few doubted the reality of ghosts, no one doubted that a saintly old person might be given a vision of heaven just before he entered the pearly gates, and he was allowed to testify about the wonders of heaven to those who had to wait a bit longer. But the last visions of the damned were longer remembered. Children were scared for weeks after they heard a story of how some old reprobate sat up in his bed, yelled that he saw the devil a-coming, jibbered a description of the gaping jaws of hell, fell back to his bed, and died.

Hubert Holbert's friend Luke James died a terrifying death. "When I was in the army I come home," Hubert said, "and Ma told me, 'Hube, I want you to go see Luke James.'

"Me and Luke was good friends. We had fished a lot together. All of em said he was crazy, but I went to visit him. Luke wasn't crazy.

"I walked in, and he said, 'Come in, Hube. Have a seat.' I set down and he told me, 'I'm gonna die.'

"I says, 'Don't think that. You ain't gonna die. You gonna git well.'

"He says, 'No, I'm not,' he says; 'I've sealed my doom.' He said he was at church one time and felt like going to a neighbor boy and asking him to come up to the mourners' bench and pray. Luke said he never went to the boy, and if he had, he felt like he could have died easy. He said, 'Now, I'm dying, and I'm going to hell. I can just bat my eyes and hellfahr is right in front of em.' He was the most pitifullest man I've ever talked to."

The strange visions of drunken hillmen scared the country people. After old man Green had been on one of his two-week drunks, he was afflicted with what his family called the "drunken dreamings," and he ordered his oldest boy Silas to run get the shovel. For an hour at a time old man Green fought horrifying creatures with shovel and cusswords. He saw red lizards with fiery tongues, snakes with enlarged heads and one enormous unblinking eye, and misshapen deformed dogs.

After one of Les Ferguson's long drunks, he shoved furniture around in the house, had running fits like a dog, and saw toad-frogs and snakes and devils. Hubert Holbert tells a story about an outsider who came to Ball Ground and put up a show with snakes and alligators and all kinds of weird creatures. Some of the people who went to the show could not see anything, and they complained to the law. When the deputy sheriff came, the owner of the show gave him a few drinks before he let him go inside to see the show. When the deputy finally went in, he saw so many strange things that he bought a half interest in the show.

Some of the living creatures which a few hillmen see are as strange as the creatures of the "drunken dreamings." Hubert Holbert knows unusual snakes. "A hoop snake," he says, "is a snake with a horn on it like a rooster's spur. The horn is on its tail. I've seed one. They claim that a hoop snake can stick that spur in a pretty-good-sized sapling and it will wilt in twenty-four hours. They are real poison. Folks claim they will git in a circle and roll, but I never seed one do that. They claim they roll like a wheel. That's how they get their start to stick that spur in something. A horn snake and a hoop snake is the same thing. A joint snakes comes unjointed. I've got one over at the house pickled in alcyhall now. He's got places that look jist like plug-in sockets. When you hit him with something another, he comes all to pieces. He'll hook back up if you don't take a piece of him away. Shault Coker says they ain't no sich a thing. I'm going to show my pickled one to him some day. The one I got over there hadn't never made a joint yet. It's a young one, but you can see where it's fixing to joint. I've killed three or four over around Herschel Watkins's house. I killed one great big one. They ain't poisonous. They look jist like a streakfield lizard on the back."

Old Rad Blackwell could find water at a house place after everyone else had given up. He used a divining rod made of a forked limb from a peachtree or witchhazel. He stiffly held each prong of the fork as far in front of himself as he could reach and walked slowly across the place where he was trying to find a well. When he walked over an underground stream of water, the leg of the fork pointed down toward the ground. Old Rad said the fork pulled so hard that he could hardly hold it. Earl McKenzie, who lived at Turtletown, had a well seventy or eighty feet deep without a drop of water in it. Miners brought a portable air compressor from Ducktown to make the well deeper, and they dug a hundred feet deep. The well was not more than four or five hundred yards from Turtletown Creek, but Earl still did not have any water. Then he asked old man Rad to take his rod and find a well for him. Rad told him where to

147

dig, how deep he would have to dig, and which way the water was running. He dug a new well within twenty feet of the old one. When it was only thirty feet deep, it had ten feet of water running in the direction that old man Rad had predicted.

Hill women were extremely careful about everything they did or even thought when they were pregnant, because any unusual or frightening event could mark the baby they were carrying. Hubert Holbert says one of the saddest things that ever happened in his family was caused by the wildness of the older children when their mother was pregnant: "One time way back yonder Ma was pregnant. Us kids had an old terrapin, and we wanted to see him crawl. Some of the neighbors come by and told us to put fahr on his back and he'd really crawl. We tried it, and he did crawl. Ma come out there and stopped us and said, 'You ought to be ashamed of youunses selves, treating that terrapin thataway.' When the baby come, it had feet exactly like a terrapin. Its feet was turned up, and it was crippled. I allus believed that that terrapin marked that baby. It was a smart child. It lived to be about two years old, and was the prettiest thing you ever laid your eyes on, but its ankles was turned up just like that terrapin's. My mother was sorry for the terrapin, and it excited her, and it marked the baby." St. Vitus's dance, "the jibbers," was caused, the people believed, when a child was conceived while his father was drunk. Dave Hobgood was marked by his father, who got drunk when his mother was pregnant and misbehaved so much that he marked his child.

Strum Gaddis and his dog lived in a shack in the bend of Long Swamp Creek. After his ma "took sick and died," Strum said, "Some folks are jest too uppity to set down and think things out like me and Ma did. We listened and watched for signs and wonders. Ma would tell me about signs she read about in the Good Book like the burning bush and about the blood on the posts. Higher

Power can talk to a feller with the wind and clouds
and the rising and setting of the sun and the moon and
sounds and lots of ways jest as easy as a deef and dumb
man can talk to another deef and dumb feller with his
fingers.

"For three, four days before Ma took down sick a
turkle dove would come and set in the cedar tree by
the well. That mourning dove done the lonesomest mourning I ever heared. I always thought Ma noticed it too,
but she didn't let on."

THE NEGROES—THE JORDAN FAMILY

Old Pete Jordan and a white man, Sam Hopkins, hunted possums together. When it was time to eat a possum, Sam spent the night with Pete. When Pete killed the possum, he muttered a little saying, but he never told anyone the words. Then Pete cooked the possum, and he and Sam ate it.

Pete told stories about the days when he was a strong young Negro slave. He went from family to family with threshers of grain. Because of Pete's size and strength, many slave owners used him as a stud slave and bred him to young Negro women just as a stud horse is bred to a mare. Pete was a giant and a great wrestler. Even when he was old, men came from great distances to see if they could outwrestle him. Pete was able to tote all his opponents over a mark or to throw them on the ground.

Pete bought every old rooster he could get; usually he paid ten cents apiece. When he went home from town he carried a tow sack filled with gifts and food. Once when Pete was walking up the street with a rooster and a jug of cider, the heat and the joggling caused a gas in the cider jug; the cork popped out of the jug like a gun. Cider squirted out in a long stream. Pete shook his head at the loss and the mystery.

Buck Jordan, Pete's grandson, proudly proclaimed that he had the blackest skin any nigger ever had. The next morning after he ate white beans for supper, he said, he always found his room black with soot when he arose.

Capus Gober, Pete's relative, drove the sanitary wagon which hauled the waste from outdoor privies in Ball Ground. Capus drove to the back of a privy and shovelled the waste into his wagon. To keep from being bothered by the smell, Capus rubbed a little waste on his upper lip. That way, he said, he could get used to the odor and bear it. Bill Campton started a joke about Capus's mule. "Do you know," Bill would ask, "that they're going to take out one of the eyes of Capus's mule?"

"No, what fer?"

"They're going to put it in his ass so's he can see to back up to the privy."

Every day, Capus drove his sanitary wagon by the school. Every day one of the boys asked, "Capus, you think it's gonna rain?"

Every day, Capus looked around, studied the clouds and the weather, and said, "Yassuh, hit looks powerful like it."

Hubert Holbert often asked Capus to sing. He sang "Little David, Play on Your Harp," bending nearly over to the ground as he rocked to the rhythm.

Capus had worn his false teeth for many years; his gums had shrunk, but the teeth had not. Capus enjoyed scaring children. He dropped his teeth down, pushed them a little out of his mouth, and walled his eyes. Hubert Holbert said he looked like the boogerman.

The Negroes were run out of Ball Ground about 1912. Cyrus Horner remembers the story:

"Once they was a lot of niggers in Ball Ground, more niggers than they was white people. They owned their own homes too. Sqeeze Tight was once a nigger section, but white folks live there now.

"It was just a few of the sorry white people who run them out of town. They wanted to git me into running the niggers out of town, but I told em, 'Naw, I won't do it. That's too hard. The nigger's got to have something to eat jist like we have. The nigger's got to live somers. He ain't got no control over being here.' They come to git me to git my gun to go with em and help em run em out. I told em I'd not do any sich a thing. That'd go into court, and go there quick. They was a low class that wanted to run em out, but most folks was

151

sorry for the nigger. The low-down white folks run em out so's they could git the niggers' jobs.

"It all started when a little nigger went into a garden and got him some apples. The folks that owned the apples raised up about it, and that caused a disturbance among the white boys. Some of em was pretty smart boys, and they wanted to git the niggers away from here. I don't consider the little nigger did wrong. He was jist hungry and wanted him some apples to eat. If it had been at my house, I wouldn'ta cared a bit in the world. The little nigger was on his way home, and he jist went in a feller's yard and got him some apples. The boys caught him up, and I think they whupped him. They carried him off toward Canton, somewhere down in the Starnes settlement. One group started off with him and turned him over to another group and I ruther think they whupped him. He got back home though. They jist did it to scare the niggers out. Then they dynamited a few homes, and the niggers knowed they'd better leave.

"Most of the good white folks had some good nigger friends, like George Strickland and Alec Keith, property owners. Old Pete Jordan was ever white man's friend. A lot of the nigger men were fine fellers if they were niggers. I don't believe in associating too much and going to school together, because, boys, I'll tell you, some of these days it's going to be a mixed-up thing. Someday the nigger will disappear. It'll come through jist like breed stock down in the pasture. I can breed the horns off a cow, and the black'll be bred outa a nigger. They'll come a day when the nigger man won't have a chance at a nigger woman cause they's too many white folks that'll take it. A seven-eights or a fifteen-sixteenths is not a register, and I'd be afraid to marry any of em because it might come a darkun oncet in a while. It does breed back."

152

9

The Great World Comes to the Hills

Covered wagons from the mountains passed through the Sharp Mountain settlement on their way to Atlanta. In the fall the wagons were loaded with moonshine whisky, cabbages, potatoes, apples, and chestnuts gathered from the mountainsides. Most of the mountaineers owned slow-moving oxen; some had scrawny rawboned mules. The long horns of the oxen had tips and bands of shining and glistening brass. The homemade yokes and hickory neck bows used on the oxen were like those described in the Bible. The slow oxen traveled only about twelve miles a day, and some of the trips lasted almost two weeks. Usually two men rode in each wagon. They wore homemade jeans breeches and rough brogan shoes made with stiff leather and wooden pegs instead of metal tacks. In many of the wagons were muzzle-loading rifles.

A grove of oak trees near Sharp Mountain Church was a regular camping place for the mountaineers. At night two, three, or four mountain wagons covered with white canvas were often camped under the trees. They brought their breakfast from home, cornbread, cabbage, and sorghum. The cornbread was molded; but they cut the white mold from the outside, put the cornbread in a skillet of hot grease, fried it, and ate it with cabbage and coffee. Children passing by on the way to work in the fields wished they could have food which smelled that good.

One cold rainy November night two mountaineers spent the night with the Watkinses. They drove their covered wagon under the shed, put the oxen in the stables, and fed them corn fodder and a peck of corn nubbins. After supper, by the warm fireside, they talked about their little patches in creek bottoms. They told of razorback hogs with range brands on their ears. That year, one mountaineer said, he had killed the biggest hog he ever raised, a razorback that weighed 150 pounds at the age of sixteen months. The mountaineers paid Palestine Watkins nothing at all for the night's lodging, but they gave her a peck of apples and a head of cabbage. Late at night the train passed, and one mountaineer asked the other, "Lord, ham mercy, how do these people ever sleep?"

The covered wagons are gone now, and sons and grandsons of the old mountaineers haul produce from the same mountain valleys in high-powered trucks, over roads that are graded and paved. Just a few old-timers remain.

On a rainy Halloween night in 1940, Hu Watkins heard a knock at the door. Expecting to see a young prankster, he switched on the porch light and opened the door. But a giant mountaineer stood bareheaded and wearing a short overcoat. "Brother," the old man said, "I'm lost— can you help me?"

Hu asked him what he meant by saying he was lost. "Well, sir, the bus man put me off in the wrong town," he stammered. "I live in the Ball Town settlement and I guess he thought I wanted off here in Ball Ground. I've never been here before. What can I do? Will you call Mr. Adair at Ball Town over your phone and tell him to come and git me?"

Hu invited the old man in to warm. "I am an old

Baptist foot-washing mountain preacher," he said after a while. "Lotsa churches have quit washing feet, but us mountain folks up at Macedony Church where I belong still believe in the old foot-washing religion. I been down to Atlanter to see the Governor. I wanted him to appoint Jim Godfrey, my neighbor, a Justice of the Peace so when we have legal papers to sign we won't have to go all the way to the county seat, but the Governor was not in his office and the woman who was there told me to come on back home and write him a letter. Me and my wife Brasky raised sixteen children, seven girls and nine boys. Thirteen of them are still living, but they are all married off now. One of the boys lives there on the place with us and kinda looks after me and his ma. I've had a pretty hard time in my life. I been in the insane asylum twice, and I've had three strokes. I guess you noticed that I can't talk good like you can. We are Irish people. Yes, sir, I am just an old wore-out, foot-washing mountain preacher."

His clothes were spotlessly clean. The sleeve of his winter underwear beneath his shirt was white. Hu asked him if he had had supper. "No, but that's all right. I can do without supper if I can just git a place to spend the night. I've had a hard day. I'm sorry I didn't git to see the Governor. I don't think I'll have another stroke tonight. This warm room feels mighty good."

While the old man ate his supper, Hu looked in his overcoat pockets for something to verify the name he had given, and he found a soiled envelope which had been mailed from Oklahoma to Reverend A. L. Murphy, Resaca, Georgia.

Brother Murphy talked a long time before he went to his bedroom upstairs. He said, "I've had a hard day. It's good to find friends. I hope I won't have another stroke tonight. Good night."

After breakfast the next morning he said, "I have a gang of eleven pigs at my place. You been good to me, and I'm going to send you one of them. I'll send you some taters, too. Folks like me," he said over his shoulder as he started for the bus station, "ain't long for this world."

People in the settlement were excited when the Gypsies came from another world and camped in a pasture near Sharp Mountain Church. Their horses were covered with shining ornaments of silver and brass, and fringes dangled and glistened in the sun. They set tables with bright silver and tableware. They brought horses and mules with spavin or colic or some other disease. Local farmers traded their sick horses and mules to the Gypsies. Ab Mulkey swapped an old gray mule for a horse whose wind was "busted." He was "bellowsed," as Ab termed it; the horse could not breathe well when he was hot. So Ab took the old horse back to the same Gypsy and traded for a black mule. In a few days he discovered that he owned his same old gray mule. It had been painted black.

The Gypsies bought their food and horse feed from local farmers. They went to homes in the neighborhood in pairs or fours and asked to buy a bushel or a half-bushel of corn. If they bought a half-bushel, they tried to take a bushel from the crib, and they knew just how far to go without getting knocked in the head with a stick. Once Hu Watkins and Check Holcomb met a Gypsy fortune-teller and her husband. She said, "Let me see the palm of your hand," and Hu held it out. "I see wonders in that hand," she said; "I'll tell you about em for a quarter. Put a quarter in the palm of your hand, and I'll tell you everything that's going to happen."

"You go to hell," Hu told her. Check picked up a stick to be ready to fight, but the Gypsies hurried away.

Once a year a short foreigner with a beard walked up the railroad with a pack strapped on his back and a bear following him on a chain leash. From settlement to settlement they traveled collecting the nickels and dimes which people tossed to the bear. Where they came from and where they were going, no one knew. When they passed, small children scampered into the house.

The man and his bear camped out overnight. After dark, dogs barked and howled and growled. Frightened by stories about bears, children refused to go to the outside toilets. Boys went down to the railroad to see the bear. As they approached the camping place after dark, they were afraid of the strange-looking man and the bear in the light of the burning campfire. With a broad smile, friendly gestures, and a strange language, the bear man welcomed visitors. He and his bear had eaten a meal of strange foods such as the hillman had never seen. The camp smelled like rich, greasy foods simmering in a musty wolfden. The bear danced and performed tricks, and the visitors gave a small coin. The man and his bear bowed and bowed to express their thanks.

Medicine shows camped for a few days at Walt Grizzle's log cabin. A traveling Gypsy-like man told jokes and sold pills which he said would make an old man young and a young man feel old. The same pill could make a man wise and give him new sexual powers. Hubert Holbert and Lije Mayfield tried out the pills on an old Buff Orpington rooster. They ran him and caught him and gave him the pills, but he did not chase the hens any more than he had before. An old bachelor, Lon Walker, bought some of the pills, hoping they would help him find a wife. The medicine show man sold the pills in batches; if a man wanted to buy one kind of pill, he had to buy some of every kind that was sold.

For years old George the peddler (no one ever knew his last name) toted a pack on his back and walked through all the hill settlements. He sold blankets, towels, centerpieces for tables, combs, embroidery, and lace. People believed that George could carry an entire general store on his back. He knew exactly how to pack what looked like three or four hundred pounds of merchandise. He covered the goods with an oilcloth, and crossed and recrossed the pack with ropes. Uphill and down through all the country old George toted his pack. When he became too old, Simon Peter, who lived in Canton, took up his peddling route for a long while. But Simon Peter finally made enough money to start a store in Canton, and he was the last of the country peddlers.

Droves of traveling salesmen and drummers came into the hills on the train. They hired two-horse hacks, took out the back seats, filled the hacks with goods, and spent a week visiting farmers and country stores. A few drove wagons with oilcloths stretched over the top, and some of them took barter, mostly eggs and butter. The drummer wore patent leather shoes, flashy socks, and a coat and tie. He was a loud-talking, high-pressure, back-slapping, joke-telling glad-hander.

Almost every farmer who could afford a painted house allowed a lightning-rod agent to sell him lightning rods. The salesman and his helper stretched a few copper wires over the top of the house, tacked up a few silvery ornaments, and nailed up a bright weather vane with a rooster. The lightning-rod man's showy gadgets made a country home look prosperous. Jake Pinyan paid one hundred dollars for lightning rods. A curious neighbor asked the salesman about the lightning rods, and he said, "Seventy-five cents worth of plain copper wire installed right would do just as well."

The cookstove salesman threw stove lids or eyes against the stone fireplace or the floor to show that they were unbreakable. His price was four or five times as high as the price for the same stove at Roberts General Store or Loveladys.

The patent medicine man wore a black derby hat with a stiff curled brim and a round hard crown. He traveled from house to house, peddling a cure for any sickness, ache, or pain. His best seller was supposed to cure rheumatism, lumbago, and an aching back. Hot liniments were good sellers; the hotter they were, the better they sold. Bart Evans bought a bottle, rubbed it on his joints, and said it burned so bad that he could not tell that he had ever had a rheumatiz ache. The peddler's spring tonics were so bitter that a farmer who took a dose at dinner could not taste chewing tobacco before the middle of the afternoon.

The traveling picture-taker wore flashy clothes and drove a big horse hitched to a covered buckboard. He once stopped at the Houstons right after dinner time when all the family were at home, Pittard, his wife, Marybelle, their twelve children, and the three illegitimate children of the older daughters. The picture-taker learned that Pittard and Marybelle had saved a few dollars. The bright-eyed children, he said, would take a pretty picture. If the good Lord should call one of them away a good picture would be worth a thousand dollars. They gave him the money, and all the family made themselves pretty for the picture-taking. Marybelle and the biggest girls tidied up the smaller children, wet their hair and slicked it back and parted it in the middle. The picture-taker brought his equipment from the buckboard and stood the big family against the side of the house for a background. Pittard and Marybelle each held a baby and stood at the back of the group at the left. The bigger boys and girls stood at the rear, and the smaller ones knelt in front. The photographer spread a black cloth over his large camera, crawled under the cloth, and held the big rubber bulb in his protruding hand. In a cloth-smothered voice that sounded like a demon in a cave, he called out, "Git ready, look straight at me, hold your chin up, look pleasant, smile, and watch for the bird to fly out of my hand." Little Roscoe seemed to expect a frightful bat. Lucretia showed that she was thinking of how pretty she would look to her sweetheart. Josephine looked peaceful and Grover was not thinking at all. Clyde's mouth was open, and little Lucindy held her hands over her eyes. Marybelle wore a flustered frown. Pittard held his head high and stuck one hand into his coat.

George Carter was the first man who delivered Coca-Colas from store to store in the settlement. He was a little deaf, and country boys on the roadside swiped so many Coca-Colas from his wagon as he passed by that he learned to expect empty places in the crates at the rear of the wagon. As George drove from store to store, he slept and nodded. His mules knew by habit to move to the right of the road and give other wagons room to pass.

Aunt Ida Bailey said she had a headache almost all the time, and a Coca-Cola was the only medicine that would help her. When she visited her relatives out in the country, her headache "came on her" every day at nine o'clock in the morning. Someone had to hitch the mule to the buggy and go to town to buy a Coca-Cola for Aunt Ida. Many people called Coca-Colas dopes and believed they contained some kind of narcotic. Some looked upon them as a habit-forming horror. Many a person who enjoyed frequent medicinal drinks of whisky believed that a person who occasionally drank a Coca-Cola was ruining his life with "them old dopes."

The Roberts brothers brought electricity to the settlement when they changed the power at their marble mill from steam to electricity and built a dam at Long Swamp Creek. Calvin Farmer was in charge of the power plant for years. He tells yarns about the coming of electricity: "The first dam broke before they got it built. The fur end washed away and we had to overhaul it. I was the first one that noticed the dam leaking the least bit. I don't believe there was a stream of water as big as my arm. It scared me to death nearly. We was jist putting in the machinery. I noticed a little red streak of water running out of the fur side. I knowed it was gone. I says to Paul Roberts it won't be there six or eight hours. I says, 'Paul, the dam's gone.'

" 'You think so?'

" 'I know so.'

"Paul got several mules over there to try to stop it, but you couldn't do nothing with it. In my opinion the hole started through the rock wall. The whole thing was gone by three or four o'clock. And fellers, all that water shore made a big rush through that valley, but nobody got hurt, I reckin.

"I worked at the power plant about six years, slept over there on that lonesome creek in the powerhouse. A year or two before the dam closed down, the Roberts boys traded with the Georgia Power Company and run the dam for the Company."

Electricity changed the hill settlement. After the Roberts brothers built the dam, the Georgia Power Company paid high prices for all the river bottom land the farmers would sell them. Many a farmer sold his rich bottom land for a good price, bought a rocky little hill farm, and went to the dogs while he told everyone how sorry he was that he had sold his land on the river bottom. River bottom land stood idle, and good homes rotted.

Palestine Watkins owned the first talking machine in the settlement. Her brother, John Kinnett, sent her an Edison phonograph from Hot Springs, Arkansas. It was a little walnut box about ten inches square and eight inches high. The big horn was shaped like an overgrown morning glory. The records were cylinders, slipped on to the machine as one iron pipe might fit over another.

All the neighbors came to hear the talking machine, and all of them wanted to hear "The Preacher and the Bear" over and over. The Preacher went out hunting on one Sunday morn. It was against his religion, but he carried his gun along. He shot himself some very fine quail and one big grizzly bear. Finally there was a fight between the Preacher and the bear, and the Preacher prayed and promised that if the Lord would deliver him from the claws of the bear he would never go hunting on Sunday morning any more. The Preacher pleaded, and the bear growled. The ferocious growls made the listeners excited and tense.

Once a week old Ned Jordan, a Negro from Gober, walked up the railroad with his accordion. He told the Watkinses that he enjoyed stopping way over on the railroad and listening to the talking machine. The children watched for him to pass, carried the machine out on the porch, turned the horn toward the railroad, and played "The Preacher and the Bear" for Ned. They could hear his loud laughter drift from the railroad. He could have come to the house to hear the record anytime he wished, but he never came.

One character on a record about a mule insisted on calling the animal a mule, but another sniggered and said, "It's not a mule. It's a jackass." Some of the women who listened frowned, but a few turned their heads and giggled. "The Glory Song" was a popular religious song. It began, "This is an Edison record. The Glory Song, by Henry Burr." Hubert Holbert's aunt heard a sermon on a record and said it was sinful because a sermon is supposed to be God-inspired. Because it had been preached some time earlier, she said, "God's not in it this morning." But Hubert told her that the Bible was written a long time ago and that she ought to object to it on the same grounds.

The first radios had earphones, but soon they came with big morning-glory speakers. People enjoyed the hillbilly music and yodeling from Nashville, Tennessee. On Sunday after the big programs on Saturday night, the families who had radios told long stories about the jokes and the songs from Nashville. A home with a radio was filled with a houseful of visitors on Saturday night. Old lady Hester talked more than anybody in the settlement, but at last the Jordans invited her to come listen to the barn dance on Saturday night. They were afraid she would talk so much that no one would be able to hear the music. For an hour she sat without saying a word. Then she turned to Hubert Holbert and asked, "Can they hear us like we air able to hear them?" After Hubert answered her, she outtalked the music for the rest of the night.

The hill people were as much interested in the Dempsey-Tunney heavyweight title fights as they would have been if the two fighters had been local boys. Dempsey was the favorite of almost everyone. In his garage in Ball Ground, Roy Cobb had a radio that did not require earphones. Men and boys from the hills met at the garage to hear the fight. Sometimes the noise from the listeners was so great that they could hardly hear. They cheered, argued, and hollered, "I told you he'd do it," and "See, you was wrong." When Tunney won the fight they left quiet and disappointed.

The Roosevelt administration, the bank holiday, the fireside chat, the NRA, the WPA, and changing times brought the world to the settlement. All his life General Wheeler had kept his gold hidden and buried in tin buckets. He distrusted banks and paper money. When the gold was called in, General was reluctant to give his up. It was his gold, he said, and the government did not have a moral right to it. Banker B. R. Jones talked to General to get him to turn in his gold. Some of the paper money had gold printing on it and was backed by gold, and he felt a little better when he learned that he could get paper money with gold printing. General was a wealthy man, but inflation and good times ruined him in his old age. He made his money in a world that paid labor fifty cents a day, and he had to spend it in his old age at a time when labor was paid ten to twenty dollars a day.

General always referred to the President as "that old

King." He refused to let government surveyors measure his land, and he would not allow the Georgia Power Company to run a line across his place. He spoke of the NRA eagle as antichrist and the sign of the beast mentioned in Revelation: "And I stood upon the sand of the sea, and saw a beast rise up out of the sea, having seven heads and ten horns, and upon his horns ten crowns, and upon his heads the name of blasphemy. . . . And he causeth all, both small and great, rich and poor, free and bond, to receive a mark in their right hand, or in their foreheads: And that no man might buy or sell, save that he had the mark, or the name of the beast, or the number of his name."

General could hardly read his Bible, but he had practically memorized it by the time he began to preach. When another preacher or a good brother read from his Bible or cited a text that General did not remember, General said that wasn't the way it was in his Bible. His own Bible was the inspired truth straight from the hand of God, and another copy didn't carry the same authority. Sometimes during a sermon General stood up and accused the preacher of misquoting the Bible. None of the Baptist churches in General's county agreed with his homemade theology. Finally he built his own church on his farm and preached the sermons himself.

As a young man, General had had great pride; and he had even been a highly respected member of the board of education although he was himself almost illiterate. In his latter years he had almost no pride at all. Old age and the modern world were more than he could endure.

During the depression few tenant farmers attempted to get employment on the WPA projects. Many needy people refused charities. The farmer believed it was evil to accept government payments except in the last great need.

DICK AND DOCK HARVEY

Dick and Dock Harvey and their parents lived on a farm deep in a forest with only a small dead-end dirt road connecting them to the outside world. For years their mother lay sick in a room with no window, no daylight, and no lamp. When she died, her sons buried her in a coffin made out of timber saved for years in the loft. The father died, and the two boys lived alone. They collected limbs from trees, broken fruit jars, tin cans, pieces of broken churns, and even strings. Anything they found, they picked up and stored in their home. There were only trails between the trash gathered in the rooms and on the porches. They were misers of trash.

But the Harvey brothers were generous neighbors. They raised fat hogs, and they often gave a visiting neighbor half a shoulder or half a ham. While one brother talked, the other slipped outside. In a few minutes he returned and said, "I put a mess of meat in your wagon." Once Dock Harvey had a terrible headache while he was in town. Roy Roberts bought a Coca-Cola, took it out to his wagon, and gave it to him. Dock was sixty-five years old, but that was the first soft drink he had ever drunk. A few months later Dock brought Roy a mammoth watermelon to repay him.

The Harvey brothers' mules had seen service in the army in Europe during World War I. The bridles were repaired with baling wire. They loaned money to no-good neighbors and accumulated bad debts, planted crops so late that there was no harvest, stored valuable farm machinery and lumber and let it decay in uncovered barns. They bought tractors and combines, but cultivated little patches in front of their home with a mattock and a hoe. Many times they did not gather their crops. After the river flooded at Christmas and muddied the corn, the Harveys sometimes gathered it and sometimes let it rot in the fields. After lumber companies had cut almost every tree in the county big enough to make a two-by-four, they owned a forest of virgin pine trees rising a hundred feet in the air before the first limb. They never allowed a sawmill to cut a single tree, even if a tree was so rotten that it was ready to fall. They picked up rotten limbs and twigs to burn in their fireplace.

A bull charged Dick Harvey and gored him. Dock could not protect himself from the bull and carry Dick out of the pasture at the same time. In some way he managed to build a fence around Dick so that the bull could not attack him again while Dock went for a doctor. Dick died from the wound, and Dock continued alone to live the miserly and generous life of his family.

10

Two Worlds Meet

"I growed up in the Conn's Creek settlement a long time ago," Clyde Ridings says. "I lost a lot of toenails playing barefoot around Conn's Creek. I got a chance to go to Ball Ground twicet a year, in the spring in guanner-buying time and in the fall in cotton-selling time. Them was the only times I ever got to go to town. My father would buy a quarter's worth of cheese and a poke of crackers, and we et all the way home. They was really good, because they was strange, I reckin. I was fifteen years old when I first went to Canton, the county seat, about seventeen miles from where I lived. We went in a buggy. About the only time anybody ever went to Canton was during court week, and we went to listen to court and to trade mules and horses. After we come back, the trip was about all we talked about fer a month."

On Sundays families traveled in their wagons or in two-seated hacks with flat tops and fringes hanging down from the top. The Watkins family had so many children that they could not travel in a hack or a buggy. Joe and Palestine sat on a spring seat in the wagon; two or three older children had chairs, and the younger children sat on quilts spread out flat on the bed of the wagon. Sometimes they visited uncles and aunts fifteen miles away; when they traveled beyond the hog pen, they said, they were in strange country. People who lived ten or twelve miles away built different kinds of barns, and owned new things that the Watkins children had never seen.

On one trip Aunt Minerva McWhorter gave two of the Watkins children a cat, and they held it in their laps all the sixteen miles back home. Children tired of travel, fought, and asked for something to eat from the pasteboard box or Palestine's satchel. It contained gingerbread, or teacakes, or sweetbread made of biscuit dough with syrup or sugar added. After eating, the children became thirsty. Sometimes Joe carried jars of water, but usually they stopped to get water at the well of some farmer who lived on the roadside. The children drank in turn, and by the time the last one had had a drink they were ready to start around again. Joe said it took thirty minutes to get them all tanked up with water. In almost every hollow the team stopped to drink water from the branches they forded.

Sometimes one or two of Joe's boys went with him to pay the taxes at the county seat. On the night before the trip Hu was so excited he could not sleep. They started in the buggy before daylight, and the trip lasted the entire day. The mornings always seemed cold. Joe wrapped an old-fashioned lantern in a blanket to keep their feet warm, or he used heated bricks wrapped in newspapers. Sometimes it was so cold that Joe or Hu walked in order to get warm. If both walked, Joe held the reins to keep the horse from running. A walk for a mile made them warm enough to ride in the buggy again.

When dinner time came, they fed the horse or the mule a bundle of fodder and about six ears of corn from the back of the buggy. Joe bought a dime's worth of crackers from a cracker barrel and fifteen cents worth of cheese cut from a revolving hoop. Joe asked, "What do you sell your cheese at?" The lady replied, "Ten cents a whack." The size of a whack seemed to be fairly stand-dard. Cheese and crackers with a red or yellow soda pop were a treat.

World War I forced many a country boy to see the great world for the first time. Clyde Ridings was the first man in Cherokee County to be examined for conscription during the War. "I was the first man examined," Clyde says. "Josiah Pinyan was the second; he come in right behind me. The people then did not have radios or take a newspaper, and they didn't hardly know what the War was about. Nobody volunteered, and most folks dreaded it a whole lot when they received the little card telling them to report to be examined. They didn't know what to think about the War. They jist didn't realize what it was. There hadn't been a war in a long time. After I got back from taking my examination, fellers come to me and asked how they examined me and what they done to me. They wanted to get out of it.

"The examination was in the old courthouse at Canton, and it was crammed full, jist like it was when they was a big case a-being tried in court. When the boys all had tuck off their clothes, they felt embarrassed and didn't know what to think about it. I never have been so embarrassed, walking around there naked with the courthouse jist plumb full."

Many a country boy made his first trip to Atlanta on a produce wagon when he was fifteen or sixteen. Country stores bought up eggs, butter, tallow, beeswax, and rabbits in the wintertime and sent them in wagons without refrigeration. A rabbit was dead a long time before it reached the market, and the flesh turned green around the edges where the stomach had been split. Judd Roberts drove cattle along with the wagons. Some were poor and thin mountain cattle, but some, Judd said, were "shakin fat."

A trip usually last five days, two days to get to Atlanta, one day to sell the load and stay in town, and two days to get home. The hillman carried his food: cornbread and onions, sweetbread and apple pies and tarts, and coffee. He spent the night in Rhodes' Wagon Yard close to Buckhead and slept under old quilts in the wagon-yard shed or in the wagon or even on the ground.

On one trip the Ridings boys walked to the state capitol and climbed to the top of the building. Homemade shoes and the long climb made their feet so sore that they could hardly walk for several days. Once Bulger Wheeler's friends took him to a drug store near the yard and bought him his first Coca-Cola. He drank it with a great relish. When he burped, the carbonated beverage burned his nose and he was afraid that something had gone wrong with his insides.

Jim Watkins was eighteen when he and his younger brother Frank went to Atlanta for the first time. When Jim came back from the first trip, he said, "Do you know what I thought when I got down there and looked around a little? I looked around and seen all the lights and everything and decided that if heaven was any prettier than that, it shore would have to be a beautiful place."

Some people traveled to Atlanta on the L & N train. From the Sharp Mountain settlement they went by buggy to the small station at Gober. They arrived a half-hour before the train was due. A distant whistle foretold the coming of the great steel monster. When the engineer passed a white post with the letters S.W. on it, he blew one blow, a "station whistle." If someone was getting off the train at Gober, he blew three short quick blasts immediately after the station blow. If the train did not signal that it would stop, the travelers waiting at Gober stepped out on the track with a white handkerchief and waved at the train. The engineer gave the whistle two short toots when he saw the waving. Little children cried, begging their fathers not to get run over.

A country boy going to the city on the train often

borrowed his brother's blue-serge suit. If the pants were too short, he wore them anyway because it was the best he could get. He wore shoes, not slippers. Usually the trousers were too tight and they lacked a little reaching the top of the high-topped shoes.

A country boy who had never ridden the train usually became train sick. Led Lee told the story of his first train ride many times: "At first I felt like a worm was crawling around in my belly. I knowed something bad was going to happen. When my whole belly got in a work, I knowed that I was going to have to throw up. I tried to open a winder, but I couldn't. So then I didn't know what to do. When I did get sick, it happened so quick it surprised me. I throwed up twice on the floor, and I was so sick that I benastied my feet and my clothes in the mess. The conductor was a kind-hearted feller. He passed by and went down the aisle without saying a word. They wasn't nothing he could do to help me."

When the train arrived at the old Union Station in Atlanta, it was getting dark. The city lights were on. Never in his life had the country boy dreamed that it was possible to have so many gas lamps burning at the same time. It was like a party given by Saint Peter himself. Usually a city cousin met the country boy at the station. When Red Akins first walked out of the railroad station, he leaned back to look at one of the tall skyscrapers and walked straight into a stranger's fat belly. He yelled at Red, "Where the hell do you think you're going?" The clanging of the streetcars, the rushing feet, the noises of the horses on the cobblestones, the cries of newsboys and peddlers and icemen—it was a noisy world, and the boy wondered whether that was the daily life or the exception.

On the third Sunday in June each year a big singing was held at Toonigh, a few miles below Holly Springs on the railroad to Atlanta. Every boy or girl who could get the train fare went to the singing. Toonigh was given its name, some said, because it was too nigh to hell to be a good town. Others said it was too nigh to Holly Springs and Woodstock to grow. One of the wonders of the world in strange Toonigh was weak-minded Bill Hawes, who knew just enough to keep his clothes on and his nose partly clean. Bill walked along quietly until he met a group of girls; then he jumped at them quickly and hollered BOO. They screamed and ran. All day long Bill enjoyed walking about and hollering BOO.

On the day of the big singing the train pulled an extra coach. Many passengers made a game of trying to avoid paying their fares. After the train left Gober, the conductor did not have time to collect all the fares before the train stopped for another load at Keithsburg. The engineer usually waited at Gober until the conductor could collect the money. As he moved toward the rear of the train, many passengers ran out the rear coach and around to the front and boarded again among those who had already paid for their tickets. In the last years of the singing, the conductor learned to stop the train on a trestle and collect the fares.

Families often carried the bodies of the dead on the train. Even eight or ten miles was a great distance to travel by horse and buggy in a funeral procession. They loaded the coffin into the baggage car, and the bereaved relatives huddled together in the coach. Children wept, and women wailed and even occasionally screamed in their grief. The kind conductor passed by, stopped, shook hands with some of the men, and expressed his sympathy. The conductor never seemed to grow hardened to the woes of mourners journeying to a funeral.

After Frank Watkins was married and the father of children, he made his first trip to Atlanta. Hu was a patient of Dr. Cecil Stockard, whose offices were on the twelfth floor of the Candler Building, at that time Atlanta's most modern skyscraper. The elevators were the swiftest in the city. Frank, Hu, and their father entered the building through revolving doors, and Frank had never seen any such contraption before. He went into the proper place in the door, just before Hu, and walked all the way around to the outside of the building again. The next time they tried to go inside, Hu jumped into the section in front of Frank, went inside, grabbed him as he came by, and jerked him out of the revolving door. Frank was mystified, but he did not wish anyone to tell him anything or to know that he was ignorant of city ways. He tried to act unconcerned, just as if he were too slow to be able to get out of the door.

Frank, Hu, and Joe walked to the elevator and waited a moment. The door opened, Joe entered, and Hu followed. They doffed their hats to the ladies in the elevator. Frank stood just outside, wondering what kind of little room he was supposed to enter. When the elevator operator asked him to step in, he did, but he did not remove his hat—a noticeable lack of manners. All at once the elevator started, and Frank collapsed flat on the floor, crumbling like a mountain of sand. When he hit the floor, he looked up at his father with all the helplessness of a hurt cow. At first Joe and Hu did not know why he had fallen. They pulled him up, and he stood with his hat on. None of them said anything—not a word, but Joe's eyes twinkled with pity and amusement. Without a word they went on to the doctor's office. Finally, without mentioning the fall, Frank asked, "How far are we from the street?"

Hu told him twelve stories.

"We could walk down the steps, couldn't we?" Frank asked. "It wouldn't take us long. I don't want to fall down twelve stories in that thing even if I do know now that it's an elevator when I start the trip. I don't like these here flying rooms."

When country people first heard about the new-fangled horseless carriages running about without any animal pulling them, they could not believe any such thing existed. Many a country boy first saw an automobile when he went to Atlanta. It was an awesome experience. "I seed my first automobile," Clyde Ridings said, "on my first trip to Atlanta. It was down at Roswell, going up a grade across the bridge on the Chattahoochee River. It was at night, and I seed lights coming over the hill. Henry Ingram was with me and Uncle John Grogan. I says, 'What in the land is that?'

"Henry says, 'Hit's a car.'

"'A car?'

"It just sheeeewwwww by us and I says, 'Lord a mercy. What are folks going to think of next?'"

When automobiles first passed by on the settlement road, it was a great event. A child hollered, "An automobile is coming!" Grandparents, parents, and children ran out to stare at the strange creature.

At first many people believed that the automobile was immoral and ungodly, and they turned to their Bibles to find a prophecy about the mechanical monsters. Preachers said that the automobile was proof that the last days of the world had come. In sermons against the automobile they took their texts from the book of Joel:

A fire devoureth before them; and behind them a flame burneth: the land is as the garden of Eden before them, and behind them a desolate wilderness; yea, and nothing shall escape them.

The appearance of them is as the appearance of horses; and as horsemen, so shall they run.

Like the noise of chariots on the tops of mountains shall they leap, like the noise of a flame of fire that devoureth the stubble, as a strong people set in battle array.

Before their face the people shall be much pained: all faces shall gather blackness.

They shall run like mighty men; they shall climb the wall like men of war; and they shall march every one on his ways, and they shall not break their ranks:

Neither shall one thrust another; they shall walk every

one in his path: and when they fall upon the sword, they shall not be wounded.

They shall run to and fro in the city; they shall run upon the wall, they shall climb up upon the houses; they shall enter in at the windows like a thief.

The earth shall quake before them; the heavens shall tremble: the sun and the moon shall be dark, and the stars shall withdraw their shining. . . .

Horses and mules were terrified of automobiles. The roads were narrow, and a man who owned a mule or a horse that was afraid of automobiles lived in dread of horrors. Every moment on the road he watched and listened. If he heard an automobile coming, every member of the family jumped out of the wagon, and the strongest or bravest man in the group held onto the horse's bridle. The women swarmed off the road into the edge of the woods to escape calamity. The people were as nervous as the frightened horse. Most horses reared straight up on their hind feet when a car was coming, and then just as the car passed the horse jumped as far as he could. Once when Frank Watkins and Henry Pinyan met a car, Henry grabbed one of the lines when the horse bucked. He pulled harder on his line than Frank did on the other. The hard pull turned the horse around, threw the buggy over, and tossed both men out of the buggy. The shafts came loose, and the lines wrapped around Henry's ankle. But he held the horse. Old Uncle Jasper Hendrix drove cattle to the stockyard in Atlanta, and they were afraid of automobiles. When one came near, he said, "Yon comes another one of them damned old mortargobiles."

Calvin Farmer bought one of the first cars and told many a story about his early travels in it: "John Cagle owned the first car that ever come to Ball Ground. Just atter John bought his car, I bought me one in 1914. I went over here to Conn's Creek to church, and right this side of Marb Hester's I met a man and a boy and his family in a wagon coming to Ball Ground. I saw the team was gittin scared, and I jist stopped my car as fer out of the road as I could. The road was narrow. The feller started throwing his hands up and taking them down, over and over, as if he was praying in a revival meeting and scared to death of the devil. I went on down thar, and asked, 'Is they anything I can do fur you to help you git by?'

"The boy said, 'You hold dad while I drive the team by.'

"I didn't know what to do.

"Once me and Dave Hammontree went back to where his daddy used to live in a cabin in the mountains that jist had a dirt floor. I got over to a steep curve in the mountains, and there was their little shack right below the road. Five or six kids playing in the yard was scared to death of the car, and they run behind the house. That was in 1914. I offered to take them fer a ride, but they was too scared to even git close to the car.

"Arthur Ingram bought a car that run with a chain like a bicycle. Over here on the river hill, the chain run off and his brakes give out. He told his wife, 'Now hold on tight; I don't know where I'm gonna make this curve ahead of us or not.' He made it, but he shore thought he was gonna have a wreck."

Many men learned how to repair all the minor ailments of the cars, but most drivers knew little about them. Hu Watkins waited until 1926 before he bought his first car. He paid Dewey Wood $125.00 for a used 1922 Ford roadster, which had a red stripe on the wheels. Hu was always dusty, sweaty, and angry by the time he had turned the hand crank around and around and started the motor. On the first trip to Ball Ground at night Hu and his wife passed under one of the new electric street lights. She asked if it wasn't wise to save electricity under the street lights, and she reached over and pushed off the lights. Hu grumbled a little and turned them back on. At the bottom of the hill the motor sputtered and died as it often did. Hu pulled the choke with one hand and turned the crank with the other until he was worn out and angry. "If you hadn't turned off the lights," he said, "the damn car wouldn't have stopped."

There were no paved roads in the country, and people were not careful to keep nails off the road. The tires were old high-pressure tires, two feet high and two inches in diameter. If a man had a flat, he fixed it on the road and pumped the tire up with an old-fashioned hand pump. A man who drove to Atlanta fifty miles away and back without having a puncture bragged to his friends for several days. Everyone did his best to climb steep hills in high gear. Rather than shift to low, a driver let his car jump and choke until the motor died. When he did succeed, he bragged, "My old car went over the Barker Spring Hill in high. Will yores make it?"

The red clay roads were so dusty that travelers almost choked and the driver could not see the road. An ugly cloud of red dust hung over the road like fog over a river on a damp morning. Old man J. F. Cain and his wife sat on their little front porch about twenty or thirty feet from the road even when it was so dusty that the passers-by could not see the old man and his wife. In hot weather, people who lived in houses along the roadside kept the doors and the windows closed all day, and even then dust sifted into the home and into the beds. When there was an all-day singing back in the country and many cars passed, a housewife had to take the top covering off the bed and shake out the dust before going to bed. A child could write his name in the dust on any piece of furniture in the house.

There were many bootlegger chases in the twenties, and many cars with cut-outs in the mufflers that made shrill and eerie sounds. When a bootlegger passed followed by officers right behind him in another car, both raising a great cloud of dust, it was more exciting than a posse chase in the West.

Old people had trouble in learning to drive. Brother Jeff Cochran, who lived on Long Swamp Creek, bought one of the early automobiles, a 1914 Ford. Because the car was his, he thought that he knew more about it than any of his neighbors. He expected his car to have personality just like a dog or a horse. He would not allow anyone to teach him to drive, and after he had driven the car once or twice, he refused to let anyone sit in the driver's seat with him. No one could tell Jeff Cochran what to do. When he tried to crank the car, he could not get all the little levers and the hickeys set just right. One day after he had worked himself to exhaustion turning the crank, his granddaughter, Louise Milford, said, "Grandpa, you ain't turned the switch on."

"You git back in the house," he said, "before I bush you one."

She retreated, and he kept turning and twisting the crank. When he became completely exhausted, he stumbled to the seat of the car and looked at all the levers. Then he went back to the front and turned the crank some more. At last he called Louise, "What was it you told me to do?"

She showed him, and the Ford cranked easily.

"Now git in," he said, "and I'll give you a ride." He started out down a steep hill on the narrow road, but he forgot how to stop the car. It went faster and faster. As Jeff passed the Bedney Holcomb place, he pushed aside the curtain, stuck his head out and yelled, "Stop me! Stop me!" Finally he ran into a red clay bank and stopped. After that Jeff stored his car in a shed or a part of the barn. It stood there for nearly forty years before one of his sons agreed to sell it. A Ford dealer finally offered more for the antique than it had cost originally.

Old Model-T's had no doors on the front left side. A boy helped his girl friend into the car, adjusted all the levers, walked to the front of the car and twisted the crank. Then he had to climb in over the place where a door should have been. A few Model-T's were closed in, but only a few. The driver who chewed tobacco leaned out of the car and spit as far as he could, but usually the wind plopped the tobacco juice right in the face of a child in the back seat. On the coldest days the family bundled up and rode in an open car. Most touring cars had oilcloth curtains for cold and rainy days. By the driver's seat there was a little hole in the curtain through which the driver could signal his turns. Charley Bruner commented that that was a helluva arrangement to make for a man to spit his tobacco juice. The hole was small and Charley had to stoop over so much that it was like trying to spit through a knothole a foot from the ground.

Tal Fossett was gifted with automobiles and mechanical contraptions—when he was not enjoying a long drunk or suffering an epileptic seizure. Tal's three brothers looked after him for a long time before they decided that they would have to take him to the state asylum for the insane. Finally they loaded him into a car and started the long trip to Milledgeville through Atlanta. But Atlanta's complicated traffic and the traffic lights were too much for them, and just before the Fossett brothers reached the big city they discovered that not one of them was able to drive the car through Atlanta. Finally Joe asked, "Tal, what would you think about driving us through the traffic in Atlanter?"

"Hell," he replied, "I'll drive you. I don't give a damn."

So Tal drove himself and his brothers through the city, but when the neighbors heard the story, they laughed and said they believed the Fossett boys left the wrong one in the state asylum.

General Wheeler was a middle-aged man when he bought his first automobile. For a few years after the cars came he drove his "yaller" mule, old Punkin. The red-wheeled buggy squirted down the river hill at dangerous speeds while General whipped for greater speed or sawed back on the bit. General never owned a horse because he said horses were not good to plow. He liked a mule and buggy, and he wanted his mules to be able to outrun any other mules in the settlement. When General finally gave in to his sons and bought a Model-T, he still kept old Punkin. Independent as the mule was, he was more controllable than the Ford. On days when General went to town in the car, old one-eyed Tom Wilson could hear the motor racing from his field a mile and a half away.

When General was in his fifties, he had a boyish, teen-age exuberance with his automobile. He took great pride in its speed and his driving. One day General started to town with his son Cece, who knew how to drive. Cece gave his father instructions: "Dad, you just ain't doing this right. You're driving too fer out of the road and too close to the ditch."

"Who's a-driving?" General asked. Just at that moment he forgot that the curtain was up, cleared his throat, and spit on the curtain. In his excitement he did not take time to get out his handkerchief; he just wiped the spit off with his hand, forgot about driving, ran across a ditch, and stopped in a cornfield.

When General and Harley McPherson went to a funeral, General decided to show Mack that his car was better than the McPhersons'. "Mack," he said, "I'm going to take you to ride and show you what my car can do." He forgot to slow up for a curve. The car left the road and ran into a bank. As it turned sideways, General automatically put his arm out to catch it, and it pinned his arm between the car and the bank. As Mack helped General free himself, he said, "You shore have got a good car here, General. Our'n ain't never been able to do something like this."

No matter how many times General traded cars, he always thought the car he was trading in had not lost any value. If he bought a car for eight hundred dollars and then traded it in on another eight-hundred-dollar car, he figured that the second car had cost him sixteen hundred. By the time he sold his last car, it was worth thousands even when a new car cost only seven hundred. "That shittin Shivalay," he would say, "cost me five thousand dollars, jist like it is." General never changed the oil in his car; sometimes he would add water. His car, he said, had run forty thousand miles on a gallon of oil. He did not know that one of his sons sometimes changed the oil without letting him know about it. General thought his car ought to have as much personality as a mule.

The bed of the old road leading from the highway to the old Cherry Grove settlement has been slowly lowered between its banks by erosion and travel. It crosses a narrow bridge over Long Swamp Creek, runs straight through the flat bottom land, then begins its crooked windings back into the red hills.

Almost all the land has been bought by a pulpwood company. Old fields are covered by pines. Most of the people are gone, and houses have been torn down or allowed to rot. In the old days the Holcombs, Cochrans, Lawsons, Moodys, Wheelers, Ridings, Byerses, and Beards had well-kept homes and hillside farms. Now Cherry Grove is a ghost community.

The Browns have held on to their hilly farm of eighty acres. Janie and Brutus have never married, and they live in a three-room house with their brother Gorman and his wife. Janie, the oldest, says she has passed the allotted time of three score and ten which the Lord promised. The one chimney at the end of the house is made of rough stones held together by red clay mud. In the front yard are red touch-me-not flowers and a pile of firewood. The Browns own no modern gadget of any kind: no television, refrigeration, telephone, electricity, or automobile. The floors are made of unpainted pine boards. The bedsteads are the same old iron beds used by their father and mother.

Gorman says their crops this year are "purty porely, and the peas are the little old knotty kind and so wormy it's hard to gather a mess to eat." Since the neighbors have moved away, foxes, coons, and possums are taking over; Gorman says the coons are eating up the corn. He "sot" a steel trap to catch the coons. When he went to the trap one morning before sunup, he found that the trap had caught one by its foot, and the coon had wollered up the ground all around the stob the trap chain was fastened to. The coon had escaped by jerking his foot and leaving two toes and a long leader.

Brutus bought some hatching hen eggs from Coy Holcomb to start a flock of chickens. Now when the chickens go down into the woods below the house, a fox comes and grabs one and takes it away and eats it all except the feathers.

Janie says, "When we-uns die I guess nobody else will ever live here, and we are a gittin old. Sister Mellie died seven years ago. She had a cancer or tumor and her chest jist caved in. I have a bad gall bladder, and my liver gives me a heap of trouble. Brutus he's fifty-nine years old and old enough to be married, but he ain't strong. We ain't got no uncles or folks except cousins on Pa's and Ma's sides, and they are scattered here and yon in Acworth, Nelson, Mayetter. One of our preacher-cousins lives in Cyartersville. We all belong to Conn's Creek Church, but not many folks go thar any more. It's mighty sad, but I guess this country is jist dying out."

AUNT CORA WHEELER

Aunt Cora was frail and thin. Her arms were almost the same size from her hands to her shoulders, and her legs were as straight as a pole. After she was twenty-five or thirty, her hair was white as a snowbank, and no one believed that she had ever been young.

She never knew anything but poverty and hard work. From childhood she helped her mother, who was blind, and took care of her father, a fierce little man with a pointed black beard. At seventeen she fell in love with a young man traveling through the settlement. They were married two weeks later, but two months after the wedding he walked away without a word or a reason and she never heard from him again in her eighty-five years. She had loved her husband. After he left, she seemed afraid of men. She would not look at a man who was not a member of her family.

After her father and mother died she earned enough to buy herself a little sugar, coffee, sidemeat, and tobacco. Without a plow she tilled a few rows of corn, beans, and peas. For decades she carried in her bosom a little money she was saving to pay for her burial.

Her little body grew weaker and smaller. In her old age weakness made her weave from side to side when she walked seven miles to Ball Ground to trade at Roberts Store. In the last two or three years of her life a distant relative helped her to get an old-age pension. But Aunt Cora went to see Louvelle Lawson, the welfare lady of the county, and asked to be taken off the pension list because somebody else might need the money more than she did.

She laughed quickly and quietly, and her hands were always in motion, fluttering a little like a bird. When some of her family asked her to live with them, she stayed a couple of days until she knew she could leave without hurting their feelings. Then she walked home.

In death Aunt Cora became a peaceful old lady in a cheap casket, paid for by the little money she carried for decades in her bosom. One of her country neighbors bought her a tombstone and composed her epitaph himself. "Lonely tired traveler home from her journey."